FISHING TIPS AND TALES

IAN JONES & LEE VERNON

Cover Design: i2i Design Pty Ltd
Illustration: Monitor Graphics
Editor: Samantha McCrow

Published in 2004 by Hinkler Books Pty Ltd
17–23 Redwood Drive
Dingley VIC 3172 Australia
www.hinklerbooks.com

© Hinkler Books Pty Ltd 2004

Reprinted 2004

All rights reserved. No part of this publication may be reproduced, stored in a retrieval system, or transmitted in any way or by any means, electronic, mechanical, photocopying, recording or otherwise, without the prior written permission of the copyright holders.

ISBN 1 7412 1654 0
Printed and bound in Australia

CONTENTS

Introduction   v
Getting Started   1
    Rods   2
    Reels   5
    Hooks   10
    Sinkers   17
    Swivels   21
    Lines   24
    Rigs   28
    Tackle Tips   35
    'Do It Yourself' Ideas   50
    Other Equipment   53

The Fishing Trip   68
    Who to Take Fishing?   69
    Baits and Lures   76

FISHING TIPS AND TALES

Fishing without Success	109
Fishing Knots and Ties	115
Buying a Boat	146
The Aborted Fishing Trip	150
The Family Outing	156
Trout Fishing	160
Fishing with Women	166

Where to Fish 174

Fishing from Boats	174
Rock Fishing	184
Fishing the Beach	187
Fishing in Bays and Inlets	191
Game Fishing	193
Pier Fishing	200
More Tips on Finding Fish	206
Get the Fish You Want	211

Practicalities 217

Rules and Regulations	217
Fishing Safety	221
Releasing Fish	225
Preparing Fish for the Table	227

Recipes 234
Final Word 286

INTRODUCTION

When I was a child I couldn't wait until I was old enough to fish like my big brothers. So I didn't. I made a fishing rod from a long stick that I found in the back paddock, tied on a piece of string, took some bread for bait, and went fishing for eels in Dandenong Creek. (I believed them a delicacy at the time.)

Since then I have fished in some great places in Australia and caught some awesome (and ordinary) fish: from barramundi in the Daly River and flathead in Port Phillip to hammerheads in Broome's Roebuck Bay.

FISHING TIPS AND TALES

I love fishing. It's a simple sport and pastime that encompasses everything I enjoy in life — serenity, sunshine, scenery, remote places, great people and interesting stories.

No matter how much you fish, you can always discover more about fishing. And if you've never fished at all, you'll quickly find out that fishing is one sport that can bring you a lifetime of enjoyment and challenge.

Included in this book are some of my best fishing tips, suggestions and stories. I hope you'll find the information helpful and entertaining. As we all know, fishermen need a good sense of humour!

So sit back, relax, even dangle a line, and enjoy *Fishing Tips and Tales*.

GETTING STARTED

If you're just starting out, you may be tempted to buy as much fishing gear as possible. Before you rush out, think about where you intend to fish and how often. A good rule is to buy good equipment from the outset and add to it as you go. In this chapter we'll look at basic fishing equipment and how to get the best from it.

RODS

Rods vary according to length, material, flexibility, taper, ring size, spacing and, of course, quality and price. So which rod to choose? Three things will determine your decision:

- **Use.** Do you fish on clean beaches, off rocks or piers, or in estuaries? Do you intend to fish for small fish like flounder and mackerel or whoppers like cod and bass?

- **Casting style.** What is your particular style – lay back, pendulum, backcast, overhead lob?

- **Physical attributes.** Are you tall or short, strong or weak, fast or slow?

GETTING STARTED

TIPS FOR CHOOSING RODS

- It's a good idea to have several rods: one long-distance beach rod, a stout rod for the pier and rockwork, and a light-spinning rod for small species. (Rods make excellent Christmas presents.)

- Many anglers have old rods they never use; borrow them to see what suits you best.

- The rod length increases the arc and distance cast, but if you can't carry the thing down the pier it's not functional.

- Flexible rods bend easier and send sinkers flying.

- Rings reduce distance due to friction but spread out the load when reeling in.

- If you are intending to fish from a pier with a long drop into the water, use a stiff short rod (most fish will be directly underneath anyway).

FISHING TIPS AND TALES

- Smaller species give better sport on light tackle.

- Buy your rod from a shop where the staff know their stuff. (If you're asked, 'How much do you want to spend?', feel nervous.)

- For better service and results, find a shop where the owner is a local angler who knows the local fishing conditions, or at least something about fishing.

- Don't expect your new rod to suddenly enable you to cast 150m. It won't. The reason few anglers can cast more than 100m has nothing to do with their rod. If you want distance, get some tuition and be prepared to practice. Some dealers offer casting tuition.

GETTING STARTED

REELS

When it comes to reels, the question is: multiplier or fixed spool?

MULTIPLIERS

In the hands of a good caster, multipliers give the greatest distance and have the most power on the retrieve. Casting with a multiplier is more satisfying because of the extra skill required.

The down side is they are difficult to cast, sometimes resulting in that wonderfully annoying 'bird's nest' (tangled) effect with your line that is caused by the spool spinning faster that the sinker is flying. Some models are more temperamental than others. All will need adjusting if you change the weight cast.

To make things easier, use the brakes (if the reel has them), and reduce the number as you become more confident. Be warned: it is essential to stop the reel spinning the second the sinker hits the water.

FIXED-SPOOL REELS

Fixed spool reels are almost foolproof to cast. Most come with a spare spool, so two different strength lines can be used. Unlike multipliers, it is not essential to stop the line when the sinker hits the water. Because of this, they are better for night fishing. They also have a quicker retrieve than multipliers, making them useful for fishing over rough ground. Their lack of power should not be a major problem; use the rod to play the fish not the reel.

The downside is that because the spool doesn't spin, it causes friction, with the line rubbing against the top of the spool. This reduces the distance it can be cast (though some anglers report little change in distance when switching from one style to the next). If you intend using a fixed spool, lifting a fish out of the

GETTING STARTED

water and winching it 10m onto the pier can be a strain.

ROD REST/HOLDER

There are two basic types of rod holders: the tripod and the spike. A spike is pushed into the sand and holds the rod higher, lifting the line above the water. Spikes are unsuitable for hard surfaces; a tripod is more stable and adaptable. Laying your rod and reel down on the sand is an unforgivable sin and you fully deserve the damage it causes.

TACKLE BOX

A tackle box is essential for any fishing trip. There are two varieties: a seat box and the compartment box. Seat boxes are easier to carry and can accommodate large items such as a drink flask. Compartment boxes are the best for storing spare terminal tackle at home. If you can't find a compartment box you like, visit your local hardware store and buy a toolbox.

FISHING TIPS AND TALES

Never load up your tackle box with more than you need for a day's fishing – except when someone else is carrying it!

TIPS FOR CASTING

- Long-distance casting with revolving-spool or fixed-spool reels requires a long rod. Some of the distances achieved with 4m surf fishing rods are remarkable. The lengths of surf rods also enable the angler to keep the line from washing about in the shore breaks. As in a good golf swing, surf casting from the beach requires timing and practice.

- Bait-casting rods of 2.2m are increasingly popular with barramundi fishers. It is believed the extra distances achieved can increase the catch.

- When using overhead or bait-casting reels it's a good idea to have a couple of warm-up casts (on dry land if necessary) with the spool speed

GETTING STARTED

set slow, otherwise you risk the reel overrunning and causing a backlash or 'bird's nest' of tangled line. If this happens, do not thread the end of the line through loops; instead, find the major loops and pull them free with a fishhook.

- Always fill the spools of all types of bait caster and fixed spools with line to within 1mm of the top. This helps achieve the maximum casting distance with all reels.

FISHING TIPS AND TALES

HOOKS

Hooks come in a wide range of sizes, from tiny beaks to the monsters used by shark fishermen. Why so many? Fish have a wide variety of mouth sizes and teeth distribution. Each hook has a slightly different use, although the same hook can catch a variety of fish.

Hooks also have a very confusing numbering system (see boxed text).

GETTING STARTED

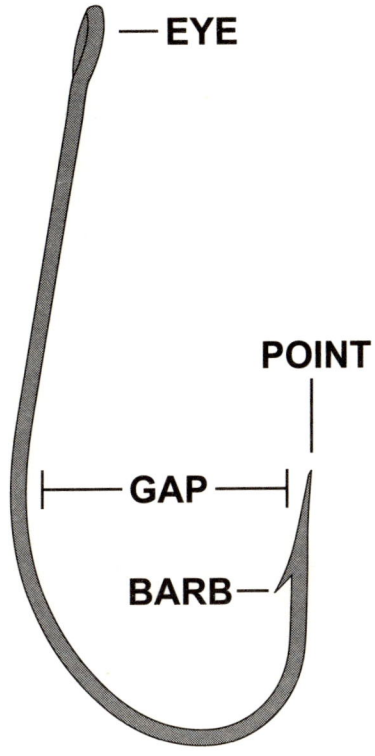

MY THEORY ABOUT HOOK NUMBERING

A long, long time ago, four blokes convinced their wives that they deserved a weekend fishing trip. At the time, the wives fully expected their husbands to fall off the edge of the earth and never return, so they readily gave their permission for the trip.

While on the fishing trip, the four friends started to think about all their famous friends back home who were inventing things. You know, that show-off Newton and that smart arse Plato.

The friends got so drunk during their discussion that they decided to invent something very important themselves.

'Why not number all our fishing hooks?', suggested one.

GETTING STARTED

'What an excellent idea', the others replied.

The ancient anglers wanted a different system to Pythagoras, who was a real know-it-all when it came to numbers and number sequences. Unable to come up with a system straight away, they kept drinking and discussing their options. When they were completely drunk, they came upon the best idea ever, which they truly believed made as much sense as Newton's theory about relativity.

A hook size – the distance between the point and the shank – starts from an arbitrary midpoint, an abstract Size 0. From this point, to increase the size of the hook, you buy Size 1/0, 2/0, 3/0, etc. To decrease the size of the hook you purchase Size 1, 2, 3, etc. Therefore, the difference between the gap measurement of a Size 1 and a Size 1/0 is negligible, but the difference between a size 6 and a 6/0 is huge.

FISHING TIPS AND TALES

TYPES OF HOOKS

Kendal Kirby: a straight shank hook with a ball eye – for worms, slices of fish bait and shrimp.

Beak (or Suicide): a hook with a turned-up eye – for small live bait and pieces of fish bait.

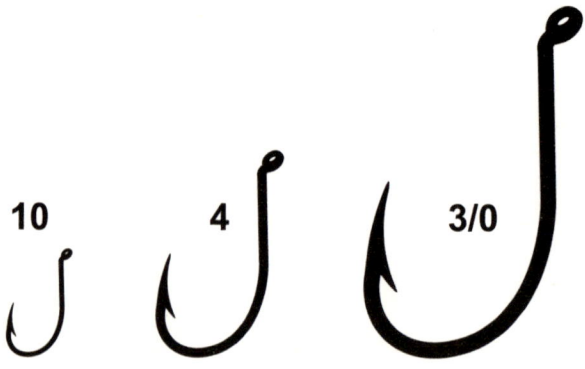

GETTING STARTED

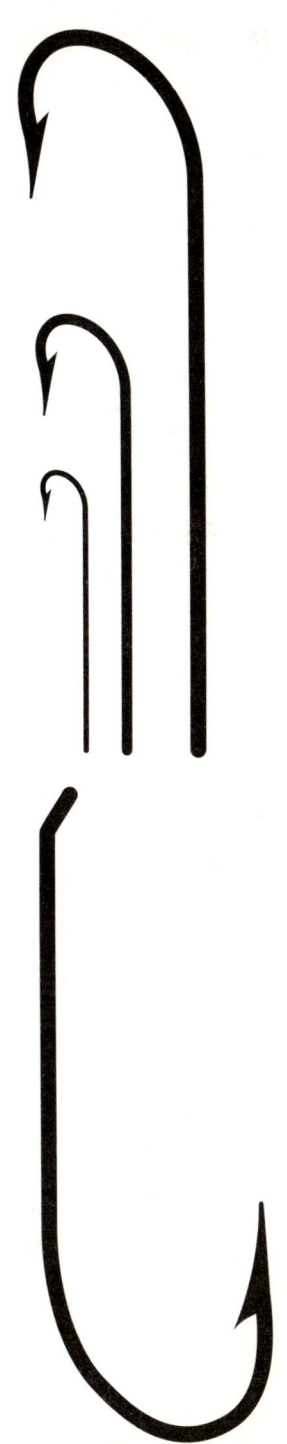

Carlyle: similar to the Kendal Kirby – suitable for whiting with worms, mulloway with beach worms, and flathead with large fillets of fish bait.

Mustad 4200 or 4202: popular for ganging for pilchards and garfish. The 4200 needs the eye to be opened, while 4202 has the eye opened ready to close after linking each hook.

FISHING TIPS AND TALES

TIPS FOR CHOOSING HOOKS

- Maximize your chances of a good catch by starting with the best option, even if it's all down hill from there.

- Thin hooks are popular because they penetrate better and hold the fish on the bend. They are definitely easier to cut through when necessary.

- Don't buy too many.

- Keep hooks in a tightly closed box and only take enough for a day's fishing – salt water is corrosive.

- Use carborundum stone to sharpen hooks. Hooks can never be too sharp.

- Before baiting up, check how sharp your hook is by scratching it with your thumbnail. Sharpen if necessary.

- Be prepared to discard hooks when they're past it.

GETTING STARTED

SINKERS

Everyone has a different idea about sinkers (and football teams, religion and politics). Decide what works best for you by trial and error. All sinkers come in a variety of weights, from a few grams to almost 1kg.

TIPS FOR CHOOSING SINKERS

- **All-round option**: a torpedo or barrel-shaped sinker is good. It can be cast the farthest and can easily roll into gullies and won't get snagged as much as other sinkers.

- **Freshwater fishing**: use a ball, barrel, or conical sinker.

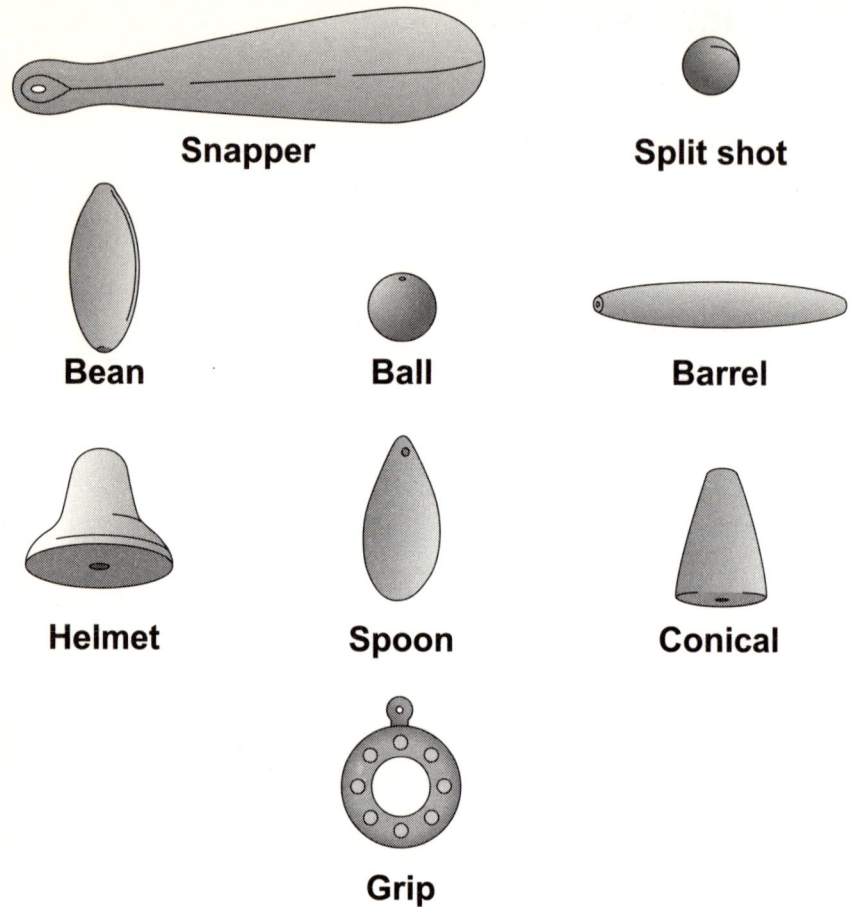

- **Beach fishing**: use a ball sinker, or try a helmet or grip in choppier conditions.

- **Estuaries**: try ball, barrel and conical plus some bean sinkers.

GETTING STARTED

- **Rock fishing**: use snapper or spoon sinkers.

- **Bottom fishing**: go for a ball – they're suitable for use with a wide range of baits.

- **Floats**: stick to a ball or barrel.

TIPS FOR SINKERS

- When it is necessary to use a sinker, choose the lightest possible weight.

- A sinker should never interfere with the feel of a line; fish will not take your bait if they feel the drag of a heavy sinker.

- A sinker should still enable the line to move without restriction in any current. When used with a float, the sinker should not spoil the balance of the float.

- Don't clamp your split shot sinkers too tightly. It will weaken the line.

FISHING TIPS AND TALES

- Lightweights come to the surface quickly; they don't get caught on the retrieve but they roll around more and may get stuck then.

- Grip leads should only break away easily when tugged hard.

- Drilled bullet leads and barrel leads are handy to add extra weight to spinners.

GETTING STARTED

SWIVELS

Swivels prevent the line from getting twisted, a problem that occurs with fixed-spool reels. They are particularly helpful when using a threadline or sidecast reel. A link swivel can be used to attach the lead; this allows it to roll around and means it can be changed easily. Make sure it's strong enough to withstand casting.

Swivels vary in quality, material, size, figuration and price. Cheap swivels that break can mean lost fish. Choose the best quality swivel for the job.

TIPS FOR CHOOSING SWIVELS

- To choose the correct size swivel, the thickness of the wire should not exceed the diameter of the fishing line.

FISHING TIPS AND TALES

- Split ring oval links can also be used to attach the lead or join a pre-made rig. It is important not to attach the line straight to the lead, as abrasion will weaken it.

- Three way swivels are used for paternosters and for making rolling ledgers.

- Booms are used to prevent the line from tangling but are rarely used by the shore angler as they reduce the natural effect of the rig.

- They are also useful to connect a short leader or a wire trace to your line.

GETTING STARTED

Barrel swivels: the cheapest, but the least effective.

Box or rolling swivels: cost a little more.

Ball bearing swivels: most expensive and most effective.

Three-way swivel: try for fishing on the bottom of a reef.

FISHING TIPS AND TALES

LINES

All fishing lines are rated by their breaking strain and there are two specific ways of measuring this.

Most line ratings, 6kg for example, means the line *will not* break if you put 6kg of pressure on it, but above that weight it will break at some point.

Some lines, usually named IGFA, Tournament or Pre-Test, work differently. If the line is rated as 6kg then the line is guaranteed to break *before* 6kg of pressure.

This distinction is important if you plan to fish tournaments or go for fishing records. In these cases, you must provide a sample of the line you are using to be tested. If you were going for a 6kg record and the line did not break until 6.1kg, you would lose the record.

GETTING STARTED

Lines come in various colours. The ultimate line colour would be highly visible above the water, so you can see where your line is going, and invisible under the water – so the fish can't see it. A compromise is to use a high visibility colour, such as green, for the main line and then use clear mono as a leader from the green mainline down to the hook or lure.

Fishing reel and rod manufacturers specify what line class the rods and reels are rated for. It is important to match the rod and reel to the line class.

The main qualities of a line are:

- **Sensitivity.** This is defined by the amount of stretch in a line. The more stretch it has the less you will be able to feel bites, etc.

- **Diameter.** This is how thick the line is. The thicker the line the less you will be able to fit on a reel. Also, the thickness adds to its weight and can reduce casting distance.

FISHING TIPS AND TALES

- **Abrasion resistance.** This is how much punishment the line can take. The line running over rocks and other submerged objects can wear it down and cause it to break.

TIPS FOR CHOOSING LINES

- Too light a line may be difficult to cast or it may break if the pressure of the rod is too much.

- Too heavy a line class can lead to a broken rod, where the rod breaks instead of the line.

- Correct matching will give you an outfit that is comfortable to use, with the rod, reel and line in alignment.

- Sometimes the terrain you are fishing will dictate what line you choose.

- Sharp barnacle covered rocks, submerged trees and sharp teeth may dictate that you fish with heavier line.

GETTING STARTED

- Unpredictable fish and clear conditions may require lighter gear.

- A good general rule is to fish with the lightest gear possible. You'll have more fun and catch more fish.

- 1 kg is approximately 2.2lbs. Some manufacturers specify their line in pounds and yards, others in kilograms and metres.

RIGS

There are literally hundreds of rigs available. A rig should present bait or a lure in the most natural way possible. Here are a few that may suit your preferred fishing location.

DEEP-SEA RIG

This two-hook setup on dropper loops is one of the most commonly used deep-sea rigs. It's great for catching bottom-dwelling species such as dhufish, snapper, red emperor and coral trout.

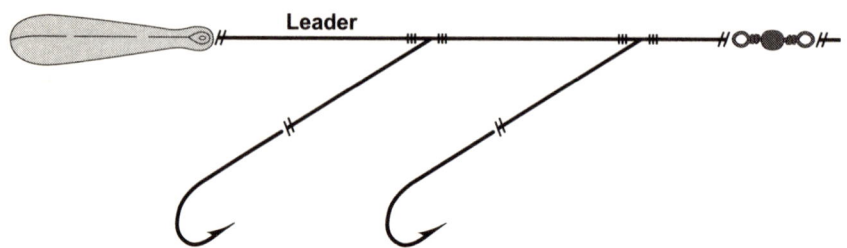

GETTING STARTED

REEF AND ROCK RIGS

This is an effective rig when fishing off rocks where the swell and waves are low. It's great for catching a multitude of small/medium-sized fish that inhabit reefy outcrops.

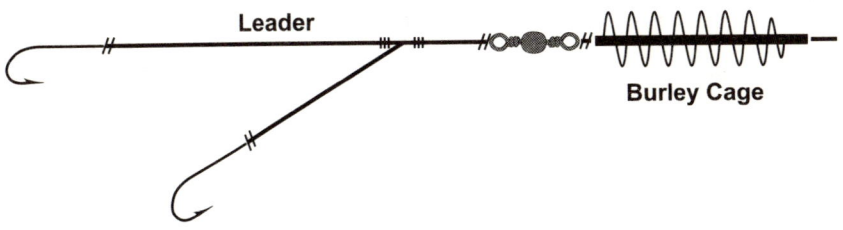

This rig is commonly used for shallow reef fishing. It's great for catching tailor, salmon and even mackerel.

FISHING TIPS AND TALES

This is an all-purpose rig. It has a 40/80lb leader to help stop bust-offs and can be used to catch whiting, skippy, tarwhine, groper and any species that inhabit reefs.

A great multi-purpose rig.

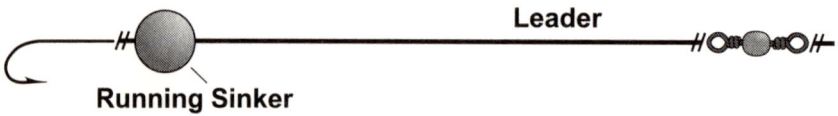

Metal lures can be very effective. The size of the metal lure depends on what sort of fish you're after.

GETTING STARTED

SURF RIGS

This rig is very effective when chasing fish from the surf. It allows your line to move with the current as it flows through the gutters. Try it to catch mulloway, tailor and salmon.

A great rig to use from the surf; the cork keeps the bait off the bottom, which is handy in situations where crabs and smaller fish are a nuisance.

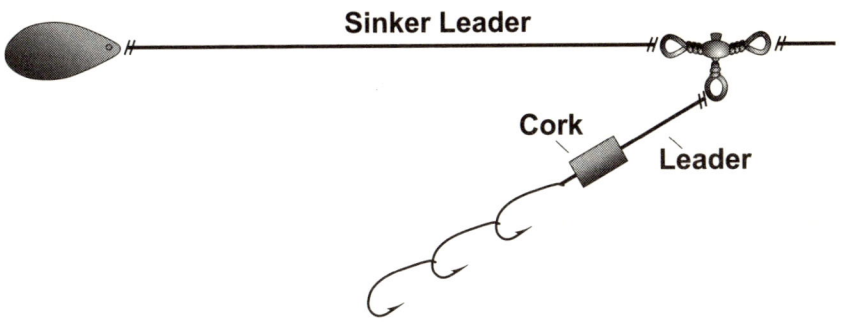

OTHER RIGS

This rig, without a sinker, is recommended wherever conditions of current and surge persist. Use it with lighter baits in freshwater including worms, grasshoppers and maggots. It's also suitable for all saltwater bait.

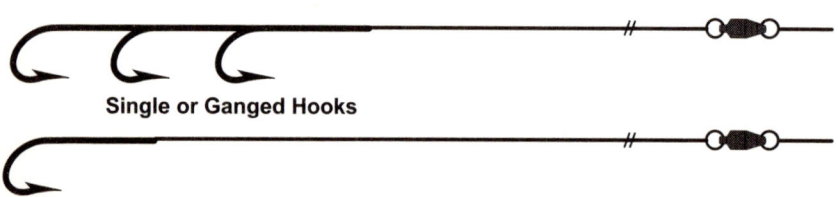
Single or Ganged Hooks

- Connect a leader approximately 50cm with a suitable box swivel.

- The leader can be about 50 per cent stronger than the main line.

- For very toothy fish, substitute a wire trace for the leader.

GETTING STARTED

This rig is designed so that the bait is taken towards the bottom when wind, surface chop and currents prevail. It is about the same size as the rig above.

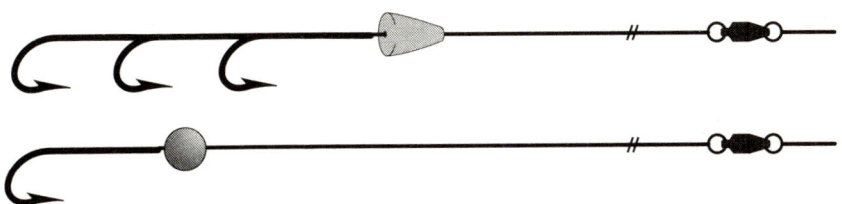

- The smallest ball or conical sinker is added to this rig.

- Popular for bream fishing.

- Useful if you want to retrieve your bait.

- Good for rock fishing when the sea is settled.

FISHING TIPS AND TALES

This rig is suitable for river, lake and estuary fishing and can be used in calm seas for beach fishing. It allows the bait to drift along the bottom.

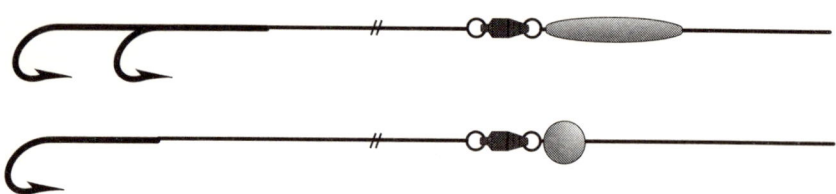

- A barrel, ball, beam or channel sinker may be used.

- A barrel is recommended as it pulls more easily through weed or mud.

- Can be used in shallower offshore waters and when drifting.

GETTING STARTED

TACKLE TIPS

Here are some more tips to help you choose your tackle and get the most out of it.

LURES

- Soft plastic lures are very popular. Aim to get the lure to imitate the bait it represents. For example, a short jerky retrieve for prawn.

- There are various products available for retrieving lures caught on snags or rocks. They rely on sliding a weight down the line to the lure and bumping or hooking it off. Old spark plugs can also be used.

FISHING TIPS AND TALES

- Prism tape can be glued to silver lures to increase visibility.

- Many imported lures carry treble hooks that are not strong enough for fish such as barramundi. Tackle shop proprietors will advise how, when and what kind of replacements can be used.

- Jigging is the process of letting a lure fall to the bottom and recovering it at a fast speed. The rate of recovery can vary with rod work and winding speed. The lure can also be 'yo-yoed'. Jigs are brightly coloured and often have in-built prisms.

- There are many home-grown manufacturers of lures that are of excellent quality and less expensive than similar imported products. Some manufacturers equip lures with stronger split rings and treble hooks than their rivals.

GETTING STARTED

- Hard body lures are expensive. Rinse all lures in fresh water after any saltwater use.

- A simple household bucket can be used as a lure container in a boat. Hook the treble over the rim and let each lure dangle. If using lures in salt water the bucket can be filled with fresh water to rinse lures after use to avoid rust and salt damage.

- Downriggers have a part to play in all forms of trolling. They allow access to the water column at any chosen depth for baits and lures. It is also possible to troll several lures from the one downrigger by careful use of release clips and rod placement.

BAIT

- Bait dyes added to pilchard or fish fillets increase their visibility.

FISHING TIPS AND TALES

- The stomach contents of fish are often a good guide as to what baits to use.

- Always tie the berley muncher or berley crusher to the boat or attach a float to it. (There are thousands of these articles strewn across the bottoms of lakes, bays and oceans.)

- Hosiery elastic commonly sold as Bait-mate has a variety of uses, the main one being to secure soft baits to hooks. Simply wind on and break off. The elasticity binds the bait firmly in place without the need for knots.

- Small brightly coloured beads can be threaded just above the hook to act as a fish attracter.

- Redfin can be caught by a method known as bobbing. A school of fish is located by using a sounder. The angler drops a metal lure to the bottom and 'bobs' it up and down. Large numbers of redfin are taken in this way.

GETTING STARTED

- There is nothing more frustrating than having mutton birds scoff every single cube when cubing for tuna. The cure is simple. Carry a 4m length of poly pipe in your boat and drop the cubes through the pipe. Most mutton birds won't dive to that depth.

- Tissues can be knotted to a line to act as a bite indicator when night fishing.

- To attract pelagic fish use a 'prey spray' to imitate a fish school. Spray a fine shower of salt water from a small showerhead (connected to a saltwater pump) at the stern of the boat.

- Some anglers use tins of fish cat food as berley. Holes are punched in the side of the can that is placed in a berley pot or suspended in a mesh bag under the boat.

- Many trevally, kingfish and queenfish will often follow a hooked fish back to the angler. By keeping the hooked fish in the water, another angler can place his lure or bait near the hooked fish and can usually hook up immediately.

- Big fish can be caught on small hooks but small fish can never be caught on big hooks. The same applies to bait: big fish can be caught on small baits but small fish cannot be caught on big baits.

RODS AND REELS

- When changing line on a reel, simply tie the line to the reel through the runners of a rod. Place the spool of new line in a bucket of fresh water and wind the line onto the reel. It's a tangle free method that really works.

- Fishing reels that are beyond economical repair can be kept for spare parts.

- Always remove the reel from the rod. Leaving it locked on the reel seat can and will cause corrosion.

GETTING STARTED

- The line roller on a spinning reel is a vital component. Check constantly for grooves and freedom to roll. Grooves cut line and stiff rollers cause heat build-up and line deterioration.

- After any fishing trip, give all reels a quick spray with fresh water and then a squirt of WD 40 or CRC. This keeps the reels in good working order and free of grime and salt.

- Drags of reels should be backed off when not in use. Stuck drags have lost many big fish.

- Car doors and ceiling fans account for many more rod breakages than any fish.

- Quiver tip rods are popular with whiting and bream anglers. If the end tip runner breaks or wears through, snip the tip back to the next runner with sharp scissors or a knife.

FISHING TIPS AND TALES

- When servicing reels, drag washers made of cork, metal and Teflon should be clean and oil free to prevent stickiness.

- Painting the last 30cm of fishing rods white or fluorescent yellow assists night vision and bite detection when boat or bank fishing.

- Dealing with large hooked stingrays can be a problem as they often hug the bottom and can't be moved. A good method is to tighten the reel drag to just below the breaking strain of the line and place the rod in a solid rod holder. If the line is 'twanged' occasionally the stingray will begin to move again and the line and hook can be recovered.

- An elastic band wrapped around the rod above the first runner is a good bite indicator. Place a small loop under the elastic. The fish bites and pulls the loop from the band indicating a bite.

GETTING STARTED

- Some bream anglers lay their set rods with their tips very close to the water. This eliminates the effect of wind on the line and aids in bite detection.

- Anglers often use a comfort lift to bring trout or other fish from the water. Gently place a hand beneath the belly of the fish and lift slowly.

- Always have a spare rod or two in the boat rigged up for the species being targeted. Lost ground tackle in the middle of a hot bite can mean time wasted re-rigging.

- Cylume sticks provide artificial chemical lights to attach to rod tips, floats and deep-water baits. They are considered essential in deep-water fishing.

LINES

- Braid lines and nylon lines are almost indestructible. To protect wildlife and the environment, dispose of these lines carefully.

- Braid lines offer many advantages over nylon lines. Braid has limited stretch, which means contact with the fish is much better. As with nylon, several knots need to be mastered but suffice to say most nylon knots still apply but with many more twists. On the other hand braid lines are much more expensive. One way of keeping costs down is to use only a 'top shot' of say 100m braid on a nylon backing line. It is not often a fish would take 100m of line in normal circumstances.

- Lead core lines can be purchased for trolling. Their colour changes over their length with each colour said to lower the lure 1m as the line is paid out. A wide centre pin reel and a stiff rod are most suitable for lead core lines.

GETTING STARTED

- The breaking strain of line is dramatically reduced by cracked rod runners causing bruising and cuts. Sometimes a magnifying glass or reading glass is necessary to rectify the problem.

- Braid gelspun and fusion lines have limited stretch and are ideally suited to deep water bottom fishing. These lines have opened up new horizons and accessed new fish species for recreational fisherman particularly on deeper ocean reefs.

- Lines can become twisted if trebles or debris catches on the lure. Removing the lure and threading on a ball sinker can untwist lines. Pay the line out the back of the boat and motor slowly forward. After a few minutes the twist will have disappeared.

- When a floating line is needed for drifting baits when trout fishing, a smear of petroleum jelly on the last 2m will keep the line visible and act as a bite indicator.

BITS AND PIECES

- Tackle shops are the best source of information regarding bait feeders, wagglers, berley cages, keeper barrel nets and many other items now in regular use.

- Head torches come in various sizes and qualities. They are invaluable for night fishing.

- Brightly coloured weighted floats have an internal brass wire that enables the angler to adjust the depth of the drop in an instant with a plastic built-in clip.

- Long-nose pliers are essential for dislodging treble hooks from lure-caught fish.

- A pair of nail scissors is an excellent fishing tool.

- Multi-hook bait jigs tangle easily. A small playing card sized piece of polystyrene is an excellent jig storage aid.

GETTING STARTED

- Hooks must be sharp. Buying chemically sharpened hooks helps but even these require sharpening after a fish or two. Use a nail file or a carborundum stone.

- Plastic bags used by banks for coins and similar large sandwich bags make excellent storage containers for traces, hooks, spare wire and trace material. They can be slipped into pockets while wading or travelling light to fishing spots.

- Plastic coated garden tie wire can be used to keep traces and end tackle tidy. Two small pieces per trace is the neatest way.

- Suction-type car roof racks are excellent but need constant checking for perishing.

- If you want to take up fly-fishing it's a good idea to join a club or take a course advertised in a fishing magazine.

FISHING TIPS AND TALES

- Simple steel nail files make excellent portable hook sharpeners.

- An old baseball or softball bat can be used to subdue a shark or other toothed species such as mackerel. (It's much more humane than letting the fish gasp its life away.)

- A garden sprayer can be filled with water and detergent to spray trailers after launching and recovery. A few seconds spraying can avoid salt build-up, rust and grime.

- The larger city aquariums are excellent places to study fish behaviour, fish species and, in particular, feeding habits.

- Watch angling shows on television for ideas about fishing locations, techniques and tackle.

- A fishing diary is an essential tool to record the date, time, tide, GPS coordinates and moon phase of successful (and unsuccessful)

GETTING STARTED

fishing trips. Twelve months later, referring to your diary can lead to repeated success.

- Rather than carry a huge tackle box, use small labelled tackle boxes to suit the species being targeted on a particular trip.

'DO IT YOURSELF' IDEAS

In the world of fishing there are many DIY opportunities that will help make your fishing less expensive. Here are some ideas:

- Make a fish-hook disgorger by cutting a 'v' in the handle of an old toothbrush.

- Soak polystyrene in kerosene for a cheap fire lighter for mid-winter fishing trips.

- Create two lures by cutting a teaspoon where the scoop meets the handle. Drill a hole at each end of the handle and the scoop, then add two split rings and a treble to each.

- Recycle a 2l milk bottle for a belt bait-bucket.

GETTING STARTED

- Use an empty 4l oil container for a handy water baler.

- Bend wire coat hangers to make a portable rod rest.

- Glue Velcro to strips of wet suit to make rod binders.

- Make toothbrush handles into surface lures.

- Use 60mm tube for surf fishing sand spikes. Cut the sand end at an angle to make the spike. Measure and cut to the required length.

- Purchase poly-pipe from a plumbing supplier and make a rod tube.

- Use wet-suit booties when on boats and canoes and when rock or surf fishing.

- Always carry a roll of duct or electrical tape on a boat; it's useful for temporary rod repairs, fuel line cuts and first aid.

FISHING TIPS AND TALES

- Got an old twin-tub washing machine barrel? They make excellent berley pots to mount on a boat's transom.

- Old spark plugs are environmentally friendly and make a good substitute to expensive sinkers.

- Put broken and discarded rods to good use by using their parts to repair other rods.

- Old golf bags make good storage bins for rods not in regular use.

- Moulds for all popular sinkers are available at tackle retailers. Take great care when pouring molten lead: wear welding gloves, appropriate footwear, safety glasses and a hard hat.

GETTING STARTED

OTHER EQUIPMENT

Here are some ancillaries that will make your fishing experience even more enjoyable.

KNIVES

Visit a good knife shop if you want a decent knife that suits your purpose. Swiss have a knife specifically designed for anglers and, let's face it, you can't go too wrong with Swiss. There are also many other good brands to choose from.

Knives will make your job easier, but a word of warning: you must maintain your knives. Look after them and, most importantly, sharpen them.

ALARM CLOCK

What the—? No, don't panic, it's not to keep track of the time so you can get home in time for dinner. You don't need something big; a compact watch-type alarm that is small and easy to carry is sufficient. A watch with a rotating bezel is also good.

When you're out fishing it's easy to lose track of time, especially if you get onto something big. Trouble is, the tides don't stop for anyone and it's easy to get cut off. Set your alarm to alert you when it's time to move, and make sure you do (see boxed text).

You can also use an alarm to space out your casts so that you don't reel in more often than necessary.

Children seem to want to check their bait every five seconds. A stopwatch can help train them to fish more optimally.

GETTING STARTED

PORTABLE SHELTERS

Let's face it, fishing weather can be particularly unpleasant. What to do? Take half a house to keep you dry and warm – hardly practical. My best advice is don't take your wife or kids – they'll complain all day. Men cope better with lousy weather. Who cares if you can't feel your fingers – there's fish down there and that's your motivation to ignore any discomfort. Here are some ideas on keeping warm:

- Wrap yourself up in lots of layers of clothes. Remove and re-apply as necessary.

- For a compact and simple shelter, dig a hole and use an umbrella. Secure it by tying guide ropes to bags of sand. (Make the sand bags when you get to the beach; they are very heavy to carry.)

- Dome tents are better than the traditional designs as they can be carried to another spot without being dismantled.

FISHING TIPS AND TALES

- Leave shelters at home unless you can share the burden of carrying one.

HOW NOT TO NIGHT FISH

A friend in Broome was telling me a story the other day. They drove down to Cable Beach and went out night fishing, which involves fishing close to the water and moving the car as the tide comes in. Everything was going well until he jumped into the car and the key wouldn't turn. Stuck as can be. His wife gave it a burl, then his best mate thought he'd get it. But in the end, my mate sat in his car and watched the water getting higher and higher. When it was halfway up his windows he abandoned ship. It was a long walk home.

A few hours later all that could be seen was a tiny bit of shiny metal sticking out of the water. Yep, that bit of metal was his roof rack.

GETTING STARTED

LAMPS

If you intend to do any night fishing, you'll need illumination of some sort. It is vital for your safety, and necessary for catching, baiting, etc. You need to be able to see where you're going. Your options:

- Battery operated torches and lanterns are good, but there is always a risk of the batteries dying at that crucial moment.

- Always carry spare batteries.

- Re-chargeable torches are good, but sometimes they run out of power before you.

- A miner's lamp that is strapped to your head is a good investment, especially when rock fishing when it's best to carry as little as possible.

For your rod:

- Small lights at the end of the rod are also needed for night fishing. These can be either chemical or battery operated.

- Battery lights should be disassembled after use and dried off to prevent the wire from rusting.

- Chemical lights are a small tube, which you bend and shake causing a chemical reaction. They last a long time but can only be used once (although they can take several days to lose their light).

- Be aware that the light can become tangled in your line when you cast. Take care when casting.

OTHER GEAR

- Wire cutters to cut through hooks, making them easy to remove.

GETTING STARTED

- Finger stool to protect fingers when casting a fixed spool reel.

- Thermal flask for hot drinks.

- Clean cloth to wipe hands before eating; wet hand wipes are ideal.

- Sticky plaster for those inevitable cuts.

- Conditioner, brushed through the hair to protect it from the ravages of the beach.

- Suntan lotion and sunglasses.

- Tape measure and scales – important for completions as there is normally a minimum size limit.

- Disposable camera – get proof of that 50lb fish you threw back.

FISHING TIPS AND TALES

- Hand warmer (gel based or disposable). Solid fuels are difficult to light in cold weather.

- Spare car keys. It's amazing how quickly things disappear when you drop them on wet sand.

PERSONAL EQUIPMENT

- Buy a first-aid kit, wrap it in a plastic bag and store it in your tackle box so that it's always available when needed.

- Always carry a camera on board a boat. There are numerous photo opportunities on almost every trip – not only of fish but also of magnificent scenery, natural phenomena and wildlife.

- Boating anglers who wear spectacles or carry Polaroids are wise to use a chord around their

GETTING STARTED

necks. Glasses can easily slip off and fall overboard.

- Tide tables are usually free in most tackle shops. Essential equipment for the boating angler in all bays, estuaries, and inlets.

- Waders, thigh boots and even gumboots can become very smelly after a day's fishing. Talcum powder can be sprinkled in each to overcome this problem.

- The popular bum-bag has a variety of uses for the mobile angler. It can be used as a carry-all for sinkers, hooks, sunscreen, repellent and other essentials.

- Old golf gloves can be turned into mitts. Wearing mitts will prevent sun damage and minor fish spiking. To adapt, simply cut off the fingers of the gloves.

- Sunglasses are essential angling gear. They protect the eyes from harmful rays and are very helpful when fish spotting. Look for brands with polarised lenses, made especially for anglers.

- For trout or freshwater river fishing, choose brown lenses.

- For ocean fishing choose green lenses.

- Ask your spectacle maker about prescription lenses.

- A mobile phone is an excellent piece of safety equipment in any boat and reception at sea is often better than any marine radio.

- Brimmed hats worn in boats should always have a chinstrap.

GETTING STARTED

- Legionnaire hats offer the angler maximum sun protection. They are usually a reasonable price and less likely to blow off in the wind.

- Akubras are a bit of an investment, but they'll last for years and do a great job.

- Anglers wishing to purchase the very best wet-weather gear could consider Gortex and similar fabrics, which are specifically designed to form a barrier against water and wind while letting the material 'breathe'.

- Ordinary garbage bags take up minimum space in the hiking or wading angler's kit. Three slits for the arms and head convert the garbage bag into a rain jacket or thermal vest.

- If you're wearing gumboots, waders or thigh boots, avoid blackberry bushes. Thorns and rubber don't mix well.

- Tide tables published in magazines and on hip pocket cards make no allowance for daylight saving. A more accurate guide is found in daily newspapers.

- Some anglers have discovered that their insurance policies do not cover loss, theft or damage to valuable fishing gear. Check your policy.

- Fishing magazines enable anglers to keep up to date with current angling trends; subscriptions make excellent gifts.

- There are some great fishing Internet sites where you can research your favourite fish, find out what other anglers are up to and send in your trophy photos.

GETTING STARTED

LANDING NET AND GAFF

A landing net is an invaluable asset. Ask anyone who's lost their kid's fish in the last two seconds. They are useful for bank fishing as well as in a boat.

There are a few on the market including a great folding version, which is ideal if you have a long walk or heaps of other equipment to carry.

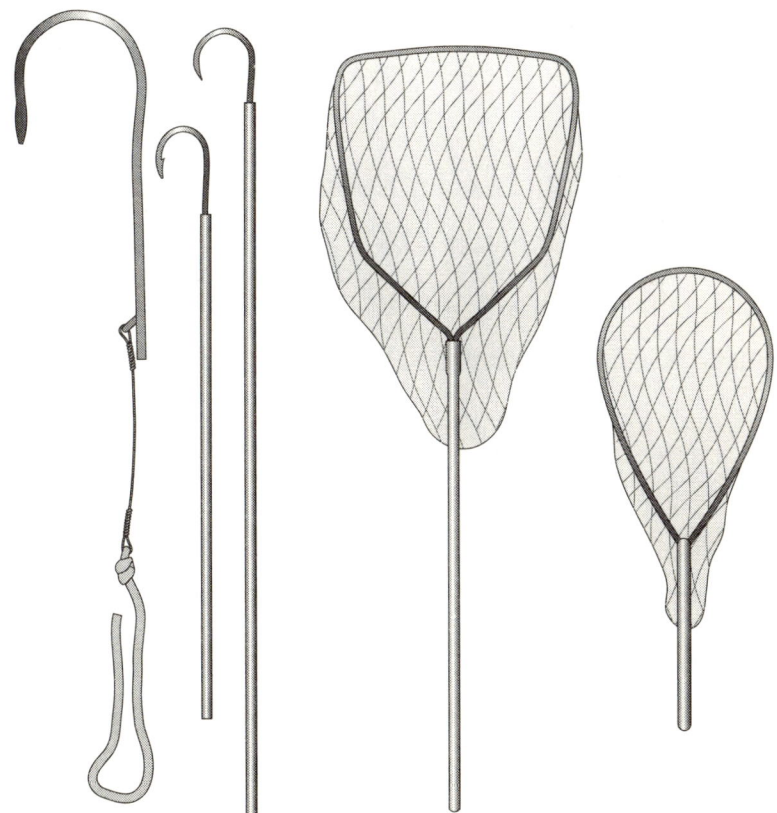

FISHING TIPS AND TALES

Another useful tool is a gaff. There are two varieties: fixed and flying. The fixed has the handle firmly attached, while with the flying version the gaff is removable but attached by a strong rope or cord.

TIPS FOR LANDING A FISH

- The cord which landing nets are made of can damage fish and limit their survival chances if released. Look for nets that make catch and release much easier on the fish.

- Use a landing net for squid and wait for it to vent its ink before placing it in a deep bucket. While calamari squid has a sharp beak, it poses little danger. On the other hand, an arrow squid is more aggressive and if carelessly handled can inflict a painful bite.

- Kingfish are hard fighting fish that respond to all angling techniques. Experienced anglers keep a firm pressure on hooked kings rather than the pump and wind technique used on

GETTING STARTED

most sport fish. This firm pressure allows the angler to lead the fish away from obstructions and fight the fish in clear water.

- Fish should always be netted head first. Hold the net beneath the water and lead the fish to it. It is a recipe for disaster to slash at a large fish that invariably dives deep and could be lost.

- Most fish are lost in the last 10m of the fight. This is the time for extra care. Slacken the drag slightly and let the rod absorb any sudden movements. Haste at this time can mean the difference between failure and success.

THE FISHING TRIP

You've gone to all the trouble of getting the gear together. You're happy with your purchases and can't wait to use them. So, let the fun begin. Think again! You're a fisherman — but you're only halfway there. You need the learn and memorise the following vital tips about getting the all-important permission from the boss to go.

THE FISHING TRIP

WHO TO TAKE FISHING?

There is no win-win answer. All possibilities are fraught with problems. For male anglers, do you take your wife/partner and keep her happy, or do you go with your gut instinct and make the fishing trip a male-only activity? If you choose the latter, how do you tell your wife/partner about your decision? How do you justify it?

If you're the wife of a fishing enthusiast, do you want to be asked along on the trip? Is there a subtle and gentle way you can let your partner know that you're comfortable staying home under the bed covers and sleeping in half the day? You'll miss him but you'd rather not be freezing your butt off or getting sizzled by the sun in the middle of nowhere.

FISHING TIPS AND TALES

Let's assume you're a man who wants to go fishing with his mates – one of the trickiest aspects of fishing. You need to make a decision, commit to it and then act accordingly. If you show any signs of weakness, you're done for. The psychology of asking permission for a fishing trip is not that different to other areas of life except that the risk of defeat is more immediate and, naturally, more heart breaking. As this is a complex topic, we've divided it up into helpful categories.

BASIC RULES

1. Do not offer more information than is needed.

2. Agree to any conditions she stipulates.

3. What they won't know won't hurt them.

4. All men suffer from some degree of deafness.

THE FISHING TRIP

THE DESTINATION

Think carefully about where you want to go. If you are planning a trip to a place your wife has wanted to visit for ages, you'll need to lie. If you don't, the trip is doomed and you might as well give up now. She *will* want to come. You mates *will* want to kill you. And your friends all over the country *will* find out about the time you took your missus on the fishing trip. Here are some suggestions:

- Choose a destination that no woman has ever been to or is likely to go for at least the next 500 years.

- Ensure it's infested with mosquitos, sandflies and carries with it the threat of Ross River Fever and, if needed (those who will need to resort to this option know who you are), deadly snakebite.

- If this is no deterrence, tell her the truth, ie, that last time [*insert best friend's name*] got bitten by a red-back spider on the side of his face. [*Insert sigh and hand movements.*] Now, two years later, he's got a shocking scar covering half his face.

- I know this one is cruel, but you could say that the destination is half an hour from your mother's and you'll be happy to go drop her off for the day.

LENGTH OF THE FISHING TRIP

This one is simple. Just use the mathematical formula for estimating fishing trips. Take the number of days you want to be away, multiply that by three and negotiate from there. Depending on the missus, you should end up with roughly the amount of time you wanted. You could try your own approach with this, but how are you going to get all the way up the coast, spend a few days fishing *and* drive back all in one weekend. And if she kicks up about time off work, tell her that the time isn't coming off your annual leave; it's special leave consideration for sporting pursuits.

THE FISHING TRIP

HOW MUCH WILL IT COST?

This is also quite simple. Apply the same formula as above: estimate the amount of money the trip will cost, multiply it by three and negotiate. Or, for those of you lucky enough to evade the pre-trip expenses discussion and who are now faced with the question about how much you spent, simply divide the amount of money by three and give her that answer. (Don't forget to grab some overtime when you get back or she may find out how much you really spent and you may never go fishing again.)

WHO TO INVITE?

This is tough. You're wife will never let you go if she knows that those *mates* are going. Remember what happened last time? So, let's look at your options.

- Just lie. If you haven't used this option yet, one small lie squeezed into the middle of all that other truthful stuff surely can't hurt. (Anyway, the kids get away with it all the time.)

- Invent a whole new group of friends. This option will take more time and need significantly more planning. You can't just make up the names a week before the trip and expect her to buy it.

- If all else fails, pull out the big gun, but only in extreme circumstances (because you can use it only once). Tell her, preferably with a tear in your eye, 'This is the last trip for [*insert friend's name*]'.

STRATEGY FOR INVENTING NEW FRIENDS

- Mention the 'new' bloke at work. Tell her about all the work he does for charity groups.

- A week later, tell her about one of the father's down at Little Athletics. (This means being involved in family activities before 9am on the weekend.)

THE FISHING TRIP

- Tell her you're taking a member of the local clergy. Of course he'll need to pull out at the last minute to attend an untimely death. (Yours if she ever finds out.)

- In summary, invitees must be: good upstanding citizens; have a first name and a surname; and be addressed by their first name.

BAITS AND LURES

We all know the gag about the goldfish having a 3 second memory. Every time it circulates past you in the fish tank, it thinks it's seeing you for the first time. I'm not so sure about that. I think fish are smarter than we think. They can certainly discern good from bad bait. Here are some of my best tips for baiting and luring fish:

- Using stale and poorly presented bait sometimes works when fish are plentiful but in the main, fresh bait and careful presentation are worth the effort.

- Hard bodied lures dive to 8m, making deeper areas in bays and inlets accessible without the use of leadlines, paravans and downriggers.

THE FISHING TRIP

- Lures, jigs and baits can all be 'dressed up' according to your imagination. Feathers, plastic squids and flashers all help to attract fish.

- Bibbed lures have a maximum trolling speed. If the speed is exceeded, the lure surfaces and spins.

- Like soft plastic lures, spinner baits are increasingly popular for a variety of fish. They can be trolled, cast or jigged for a variety of inland and saltwater species. There are many varieties, sizes and colours available.

- An exciting form of lure fishing is to use 'poppers' or 'fizzers'. These are surface running blunt nosed lures that are retrieved rapidly across the surface. They attract saltwater species such as queenfish, Spanish mackerel and the larger trevallies. Freshwater and estuary species that take poppers are estuary perch and, occasionally, salmon.

- Some lures have sound and taste. Rattles are placed inside the body of the lure during manufacturing. Taste is added to the outside of lures, mainly in the soft plastic range.

- Using the same lure over and over again can be unproductive. Experiment with colour, size, shape and depth.

For the purposes of this book, we have divided bait into two basic categories – saltwater fishing baits and freshwater fishing baits.

SALTWATER FISHING BAITS

PRAWNS

It's preferable to have prawns in your bait collection. Live ones are best although fresh ones are a fair alternative. (Avoid the frozen variety.) Ideally, keep them alive in a bucket of salt water with the use of an aerator. In damp weed or a wet bag they will live for a shorter period of time.

THE FISHING TRIP

Using a good torch or a more sophisticated underwater light, prawns can be netted with a hand-held net on a moonless night. Alternatively, place a weighted lidded bucket with holes in it in the water or tie it to a jetty for the morning.

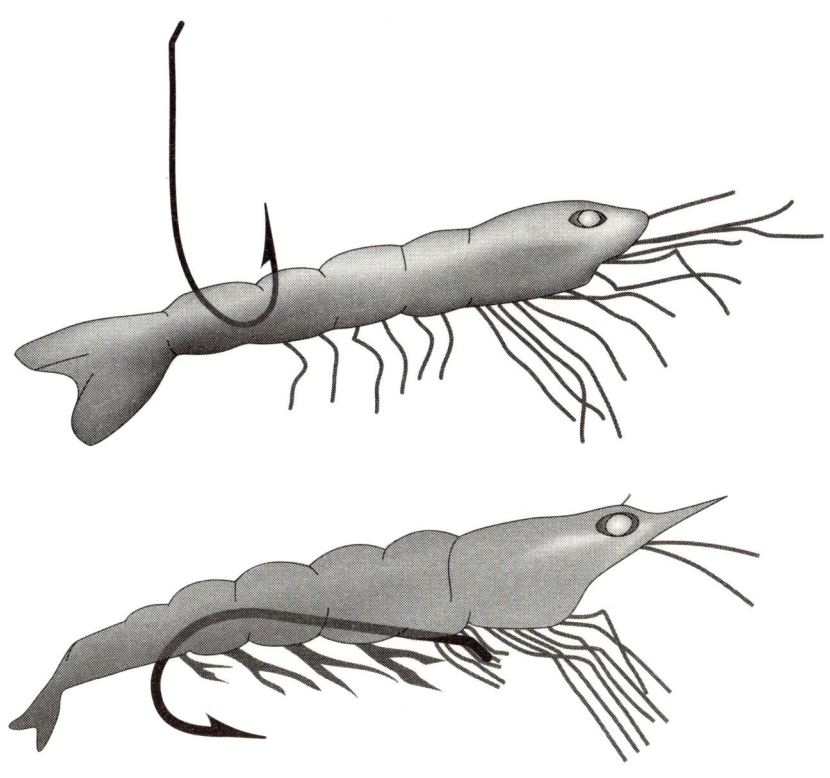

How to hook a prawn.

FISHING TIPS AND TALES

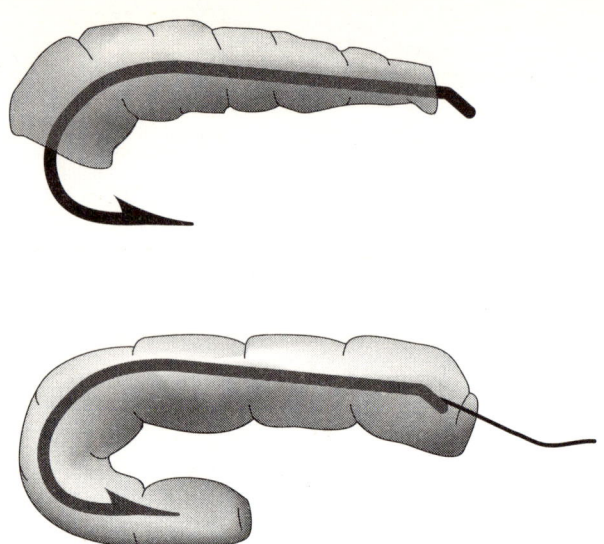

NIPPERS

Nippers are of the prawn family and they have an outsized claw. You will find them in mud areas, usually under weed or in estuary tidal flats. Keep them alive in wet ribbon weed or salt water.

YABBIES

Yabbies are also known as sand shrimp. They are bigger than prawns and have a larger pincer. They are found in mud-sand areas of coastal rivers between the tide levels.

THE FISHING TRIP

Keep them alive in salt water taken from their habitat.

- When pumping for yabbies, the second or third pump in the same hole often produces the most yabbies.

- Saltwater yabbies are best used alive and fresh but do not discard the unused ones. Frozen yabbies are still excellent bait for many species. Some anglers freeze yabbies in water in small margarine containers.

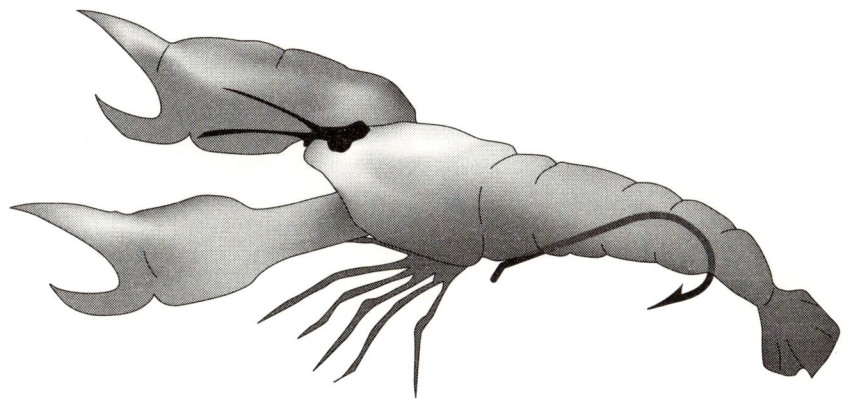

How to hook a nipper/yabby.

Some anglers remove the large nipper. For more natural looking bait, leave it intact.

WORMS

There are several varieties of saltwater worms, including blood worms, wriggler worms, squirt worms and poddy worms. All are slightly different. Fish enjoy them all.

Worm farms can be purchased commercially. If maintained, they are a good source of fresh bait.

Catching large beach worms is a skill that needs lots of practice and patience. Use a keeper net of fish scraps, or rancid fish, and let them wash up in the first shore wave. The scent washes back and worms can be seen poking their heads through the sand. The wormer walks to where the worms are seen and holds a fish scrap over it. The worm pokes its head out for a free meal and the wormer grabs it.

Keeping sandworms alive can be a problem. Here are some options to try:

- Place the worms in a live bait tank with circulating water. The disadvantage of this is that the worms make a tightly knitted ball as they huddle together.

- Use damp newspaper in layers over a freeze pack.

- Damp hessian and moist seaweed is also a stop-gap method.

- The biggest killers of sandworm are heat and dryness.

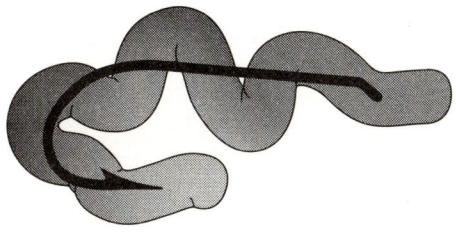

Large beach worms should appear chunky, covering the tip of the hook and extending above the eye.

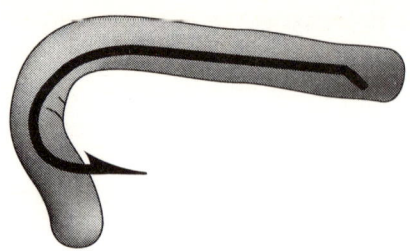

To attract bream, whiting, etc, smaller worms should look neat.

GENTLES (MAGGOTS)

They may be gross, but maggots are effective bait for garfish, whiting, tommy ruff, yellowtail, and varieties of mullet and bream. They can be kept in sealed containers in the fridge and will last for months without pupating.

CUNJEVOI

Anglers often ignore these easy to find ascidians or sea quirt, even though cunjevoi is excellent bait for all reef fish. It grows in a leather-like casing and inside is a reddish coloured flesh. It can grow in clumps or alone, between high and low water, on rocks or piers.

THE FISHING TRIP

Environmentally, it is better to take just enough for immediate needs. The flesh can be frozen in its own juices. An ice-cream container works well.

Hold bait firmly by inserting the hook through one of the valves and bringing it out the other. Then turn it over and push the hook back into the soft flesh. Excellent for rock blackfish and groper, although most fish will have a go at it.

PIPIS

Pipis, also known as Goolwa Cockle, are a large soft bait, which can tempt many rock fish species if suspended beneath a float or bobby cork. Gathering pipis can be fun for all the family. Doing a 'pipi shuffle' with both feet in ankle-deep water on productive ocean beaches brings the pipis to the surface ready for collection. Pipis freeze readily for short or long time use. Refreezing unused pipis does not adversely affect the quality.

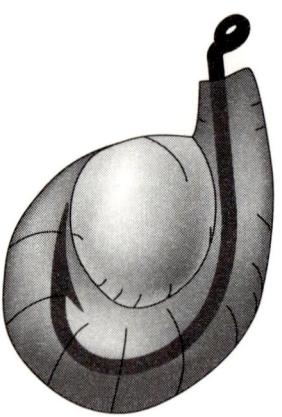

Thread the hook around the firm edge of the flesh. Bream, whiting, trevally and many other fish will be tempted by pipis.

THE FISHING TRIP

COCKLES AND SHELLFISH

The flesh of cockles, chitons and mussels etc, all attract the more carnivorous fish. They can be gathered and crushed for a useful berley when fishing in bays and estuaries, or off rocks. Opening mussels is an acquired skill. A short cut is to place the fresh mussels in the microwave oven until they open. The flesh can then be scooped out more easily.

CRABS

Crabs found in ocean rocks and in estuaries are quickly eaten by fish. The little black crabs found by lifting rocks on shorelines are excellent as bream bait. The red, green, ghost and soldier crabs are excellent for most fish that feed off reefs or rocky areas. The black crabs in the crevices and rocks above the waterline on the ocean front have less appeal to fish.

Remove a leg from the whole crab and insert a small hook through the socket and out the other side of the body.

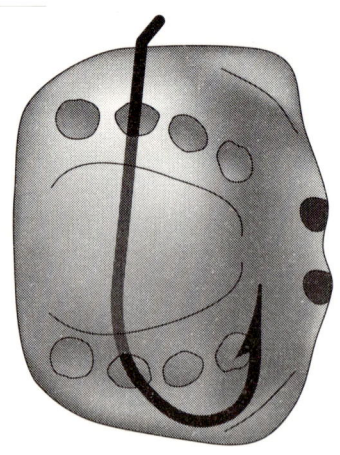

For a half crab, you can go in through one leg hole and out another.

THE FISHING TRIP

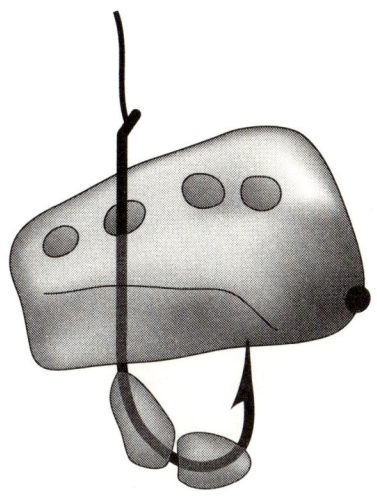

If you are using half a crab, pieces of the legs are handy to secure the hook.

SQUID AND CUTTLEFISH

If fish love a bottle or baby squid, they find a larger live squid almost irresistible. Fillets of squid or cuttlefish, or tentacles or hands can be used on single or ganged hooks to entice kingfish, mulloway, and other big fish. Neither keep well but you can deep-freeze the tentacles and heads. The mantle is the part that is generally consumed. For best results, use live or fresh bait.

FISHING TIPS AND TALES

Small or medium sized squid can be used on a single hook. A floating live squid is irresistible to kingfish, snapper and mulloway.

OCTOPUS

Octopus tentacles are tough, which make them less suitable for smaller fish varieties, but snapper, tailor, flathead and practically all reef fish enjoy them. Before use, the skin should be removed and the flesh hammered, but not mashed. Octopus freezes well.

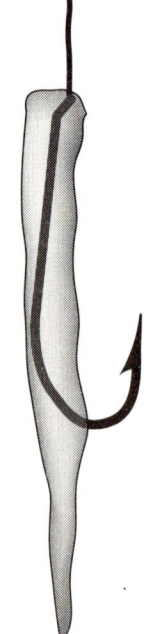

THE FISHING TRIP

FISH

Many smaller fish are suitable for live bait. Game fishermen often use fish as bait. Some small baitfish include yellowtail, slimy mackerel, garfish, pilchards, bluebait, mullet and whitebait.

Make sure that any baitfish is a legal size. If you remove undersize fish from the water you are not only breaking the law but threatening the species. Be aware that a small baitfish may be protected to ensure it remains a staple food source for larger fish. Do not disturb the balance of the food chain.

A scoop net can be used to catch baitfish at night. Use the light of a strong torch or underwater light to attract them. Garfish, anchovies and pilchards appear to be dazzled and may be scooped up easily.

FISHING TIPS AND TALES

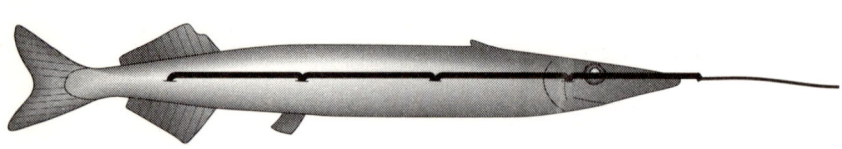

Garfish on ganged hooks. Use, three, four or five hooks depending on the size of the fish.

When baiting a pilchard or similar sized fish, a large saltwater fly can be used to further entice your fish. Use ganged hooks.

Many fish prefer to take their bait head first. Use a dead fish on ganged hooks. Suitable for snapper, mulloway and kingfish.

THE FISHING TRIP

Small baitfish can also be hooked together with a second hook through the eye.

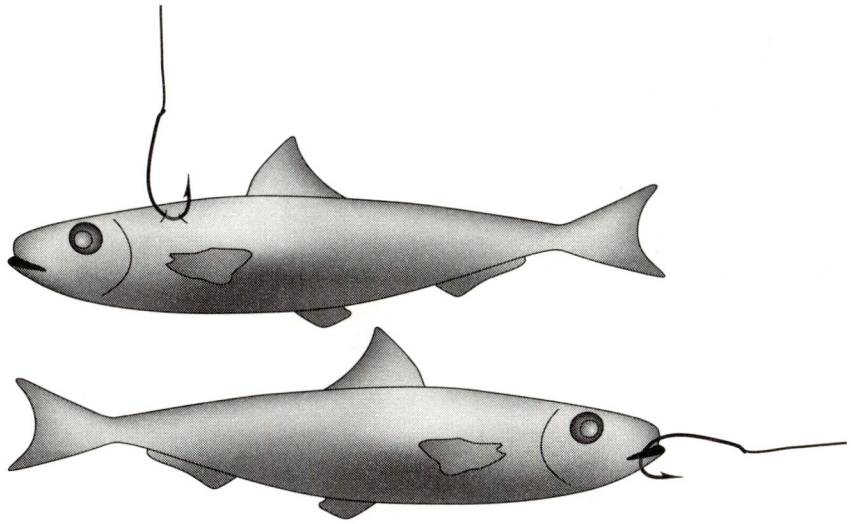

This is probably the best method for attaching live bait. Take care not to go through the backbone. Through the bottom jaw is a reliable way.

WEED AND CABBAGE

Some fish are plant eaters, including luderick, zebra fish, rock blackfish, and even some milkfish, drummer and mullet. There are two varieties that entice these fish: long-stranded grass-like weed or algae, and broad-leafed cabbage or lettuce. Both weeds can usually be obtained where you fish. You will find the weed or algae on rocks and pylons in the estuaries, bays and harbours that these fish populate. The long-stranded variety is often available from bait stores. If collected fresh, these baits freeze quite well.

Weed should be baited in this way.

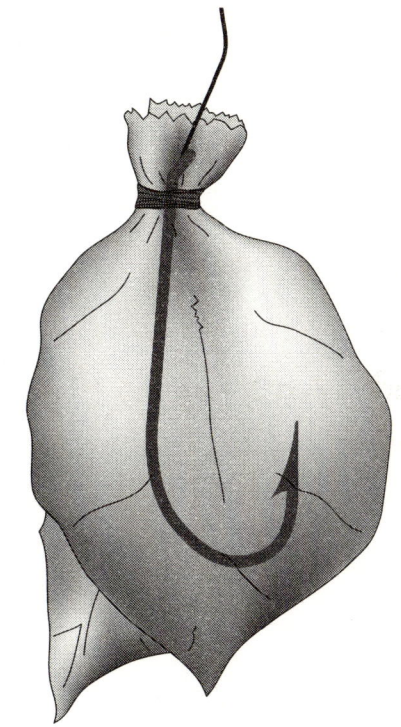

A single or double cabbage leaf can be baited in this manner.

DOUGH, PUDDING AND BREAD

This covers a wide variety of baits, including chunks of bread; flour, water and sugar mixtures; and other additives. Fresh bread can be kneaded to form a bait around the point of the hook, especially for mullet and bream. Tuna oil or other additives can be mixed with the fresh bread. A dough or pudding mixture should be a consistency that allows them to be moulded into a pear or worm shape on the hook.

FISHING TIPS AND TALES

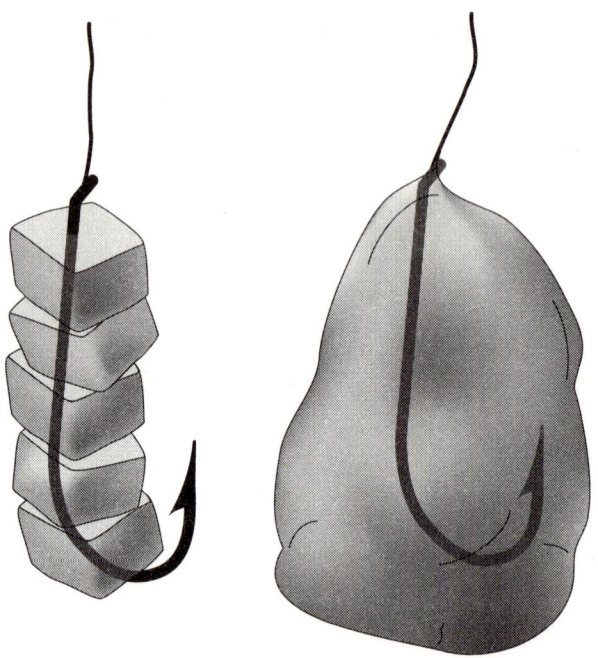

- *Cut squares of crusts and thread them onto the hooks.*

- *Mould the dough or pudding mix into a pear shape around the hook.*

FRESHWATER FISHING BAIT

The selection of freshwater bait at any given time is often influenced by the climate. Hot weather, low water and drought can alter the diet of many fish.

THE FISHING TRIP

Current temperature alone can alter their preferences. So, the good old rule of trial and error applies to freshwater fishing.

WORMS

It's a fact: all fish eat worms, the most popular being the large milky scrub worm. Another reliable temptation is the good old garden worm, while the striped tiger worm or bright red worm is less appetising. Don't go overboard when baiting your hook with worms; a single worm well presented will do the job.

YABBIES

Freshwater crayfish is another name for yabbies. These succulent creatures are found in dams, creeks, backwaters and inland rivers. They can be caught in commercially available traps or fished for with bait (using fish flesh or meat) on a line or in a nylon stocking. They live well in damp grass or hessian and leaves. A piece of yabby tail works wonders added to your hook if trolling lures in muddy water.

Yabbies are also available from yabby farms and are a worthwhile investment if you're planning to do some serious fishing.

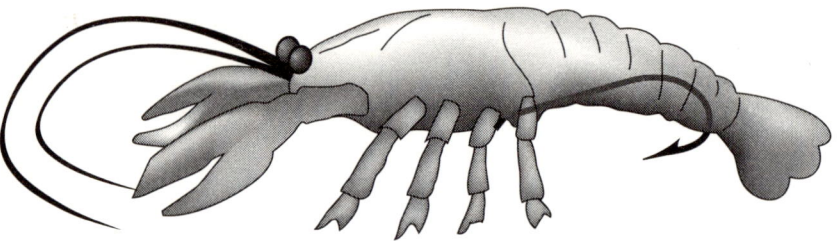

SHRIMP

Shrimp are a favourite meal for freshwater fish. They are found amongst weed and can be trapped using fish flesh in a trap or scooped by dragging a small hand-held net through weed patches. Table scraps or plain unscented soap can be used in a shrimp trap or even a submerged fishing basket. If you are camping, leave the trap submerged until you need the bait; this will help keep them alive. Stock crossings on rivers are great places to collect shrimp that feed on cattle manure and material disturbed by cattle.

THE FISHING TRIP

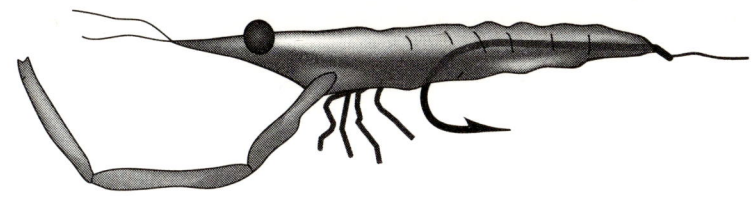

Choose your hook depending on the size of the shrimp. Insert into the tail.

FROGS AND TADPOLES

Collecting frogs can be like reliving your childhood. They're good for catching many fish, including European carp. There is no clear decision about whether the green frog or brown frog is the better bait. Tadpoles, although more difficult to handle, also make good bait.

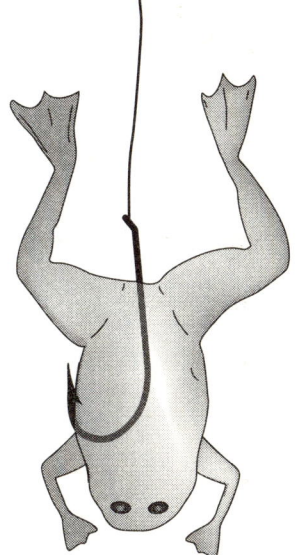

Insert the hook under the skin of the stomach area. You may need a small sinker.

GRASSHOPPERS

Trout love grasshoppers and they aren't fussy about the variety; however, the most popular is the large green/yellow grasshopper, which is actually a locust. Macquarie perch, silver perch, bass and redfin also enjoy them.

It is far easier to catch grasshoppers for trout bait in the early morning when the dew is still on the grass, especially in summer. An old blanket can be useful for catching grasshoppers. Lay the blanket on the grass and then shake the grass surrounding it. The hoppers can be seen easily and readily collected.

Grasshoppers (and crickets) should only by hooked through the abdominal area.

THE FISHING TRIP

GRUBS

Most freshwater fish, including perch and trout, enjoy grubs. They can be found by opening logs and stumps — a sawdust-like waste indicates a grub is hiding somewhere. Very skilled trout anglers never take bait with them. They use the natural baits around streams and lakes and found under tree bark, fallen timber, river stones and even cowpats.

Hook grubs under the skin. Use more than one if they are small.

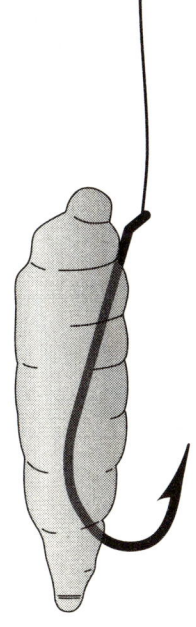

FISHING TIPS AND TALES

GENTLES (MAGGOTS)

Trout and European carp regard these as a delicacy, while most other freshwater fish are less interested.

BEETLES AND CRICKETS

Almost any beetle is good food for freshwater fish. Christmas beetles are great to use for night fishing if you're after trout, while most freshwater fish will nibble at a cricket. Black crickets are excellent live bait for trout. Old cowpats, fallen timber, corrugated iron and iron stacks are all worth turning over for crickets. Watch out: snakes enjoy the same locations.

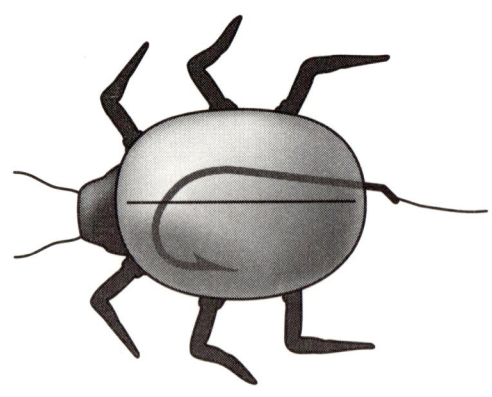

THE FISHING TRIP

MUDEYES

Mudeyes are the larvae of dragonflies. Trout like them. They can be found in damp rotting logs on the water's edge or submerged in the shallows of impoundments and rivers. They are best used under a light float or bubble.

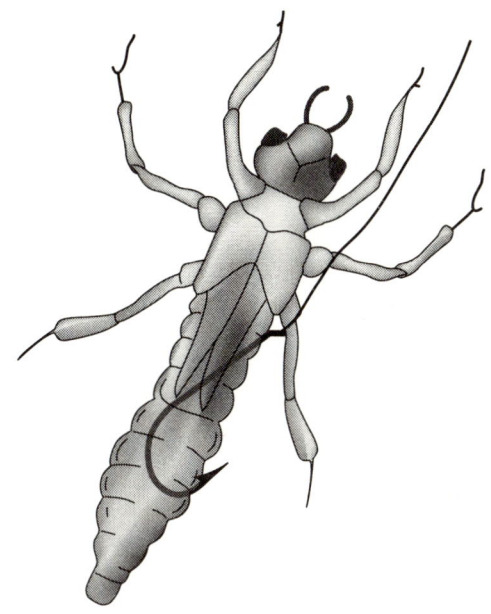

Hook through the tail or thorax.

FISHING TIPS AND TALES

CORN, POTATOES AND DOUGH

In general, the variety of food freshwater fish will take will astonish you, as will some of the suggestions people make. Experiment yourself.

A FEW MORE TIPS ON BAIT

- Blocks of pilchards are quite expensive. Leftover pilchards become soft and unusable. Prudent anglers cover their leftovers with rock or spa-pool salt in well-drained wooden boxes. The salt hardens the bait for the next trip.

- Abalone gut is discarded in the cleaning process. It is excellent bait for many species of fish.

- Sand fleas make excellent bait for garfish and mullet. They can be easily found under clumps of seaweed on sandy beaches.

- Soft clam shells can be used for bait. Either scald the shellfish with boiling water (this hardens the flesh and opens the shell) or, preferably, push the point of the hook through two or more of the whole unopened clams.

- Casting nets for bait is legal in some areas. Using a casting net is a skill that takes practice. Some early instruction is also a good idea.

BERLEY

Most estuary, beach, rock or offshore fishing catches can be improved by using berley (bait scattered on water to attract fish).

A piece of towelling soaked in tuna oil and placed on the berley pot helps create a berley slick.

To make your own berley, mince old fish scraps, bait, cunjevoi, crabs and whatever else you think the fish will like. Freeze this mixture in a plastic or paper cup

A WORD OF WARNING

Collecting bait can be dangerous, so be aware of your surrounds. Look out for these pitfalls:

- Stepping into a deep hole while wading.
- Getting caught in a fast current.
- Forgetting to watch the tide.
- Venomous fish and sea snakes.
- Sharks and other predators.

until ready for use. Berley such as fish frames, bread, fish offal and tuna oil can also be mixed and stored in used milk containers in a garage freezer.

Here are some pointers on using berley in various fishing locations:

THE FISHING TRIP

ESTUARY FISHING

Berley can be dropped to the bottom and the natural current will disperse it, or toss it on the surface to sink. For bottom-feeding fish, try lowering the berley in a porous bag. Lift the bag regularly to distribute more berley. Alternatively, saturate a thick foam pad with pilchard and sardine oil and attach a heavy sinker (to the top side), tied to a thick nylon line. When you lift or jiggle the line, the sinker squeezes out a bit of oil.

BEACH FISHING

This is a bit trickier, mainly because you will not be the only person using the beach. Establish a suitable backwash or undertow that can carry the berley out from the water's edge. A weighted porous bag works best. Make sure a rope pegged into the sand anchors it, or you may provide berley for some keen angler in a boat offshore.

FISHING TIPS AND TALES

ROCK FISHING

Berley can quite easily be distributed by hand. Depending on conditions, a porous bag filled with tasty treats can be hung over the rock face where the action of waves and wash will automatically dispense the berley.

BOAT FISHING

Farther out at sea, a berley trail can be established manually. Have a large bucket ready and dispense when needed, ie, whenever you haven't had any action for a while. A berley bucket can also be attached to the stern of the boat.

THE FISHING TRIP

FISHING WITHOUT SUCCESS

I'm the first to admit, catching fish is a real buzz, but it's not essential to enjoying the day, depending of course on the circumstances. If you're having a competition with your mate, it's essential; but if you're just hanging out camped beside a river, you can get by without catching fish for one day and still have a great time.

Let's look at this from a different perspective: catching fish involves work! You must catch the fish, land the fish and have your photograph taken with the fish. You then have to clean the fish (and the knives, buckets and boards), cook the fish (you don't want it ruined by an amateur) and, finally, especially if you're camping, help with the dishes.

FISHING TIPS AND TALES

Fishing is one of the few things you can do in life without actually doing much. It involves lots of watching, monitoring and checking and, in my book, that makes fishing a particularly appealing pastime. So, if you didn't catch a fish, would your day really be that bad?

A PERFECT DAY

I'm camped on the banks of Cooper Creek in Innamincka, the remote outback town in South Australia where famous explorers Burke & Wills met their fate. I have breakfast with the flies, pick up my fishing rod and bait a 6/0 hook with a fresh yabby (the only way I'm assured to catch yellow belly). I amble down the half dozen steps to the water's edge and do a perfect cast into the middle of the creek, just to the left of the snags. I attach bells to the end of my rod, put the rod into the rod holder and face the most difficult decisions of the day. Will I sit on one chair or will I get a second so I can

THE FISHING TRIP

stretch out with my legs? It's a tough decision. I go with one chair. (I've just woken up and don't want to look lazy.)

In this position I can do whatever I like – read a book, do some writing, or perhaps sketch the river gums and pelicans. It doesn't matter, the day is mine. In fact, the next 10 days are mine. Nothing else matters. I'll be flat out fishing for yellow belly here in the Cooper.

I continue in this manner for the entire morning and when I reach for a beer just after lunch I'm comfortable with my decision; it's been a tough morning. I know I don't have issues. I'm not sitting at home in front of the television. I'm fishing, doing something. So afternoons, when technically there's no hope of catching a fish because of the water temperature, the sun, noise distractions (did I mention the temperature's now 36 in the shade and the kids are doing bombs into the water three foot from my line?) it's irrelevant. I'm fishing.

FISHING TIPS AND TALES

With fishing, timing is everything. And now is the perfect time to get that second chair and put my feet up. With very little practice, I can lean back, close my eyes and wake just in time to check my line before I get into some really serious twilight fishing. Incidentally, the Akubra is an essential bush fishing requirement. A fly net, purchased from the Innamincka General Store, attached to the hat, will give you some resistance to the army of flies that co-inhabit our great Australian Outback.

Because I've been fishing all day, and the fish must definitely be coming on the bite any minute, it's ridiculous that I should be expected to collect firewood for the nightly barbeque. What have the kids been doing all day anyway?

About this time of night I hope to hear the sound of the bells on the end of the rod. The missus is making a lot of noise about sausages and the kids are whinging about spaghetti on

THE FISHING TRIP

toast if I don't catch 'just one fish' for dinner. I whack another yabby on the hook and the sound of bells has everyone running to the bank to check my progress. I tell them, 'any minute now' and ask for another beer.

The missus burns the sausages and I eat mine in bread down by the water. There was some mention of the dishes.

About 8pm the missus sends the kids to bed and I decide it's time for us to spend some quality time together. I'd hate to upset her. I take the fishing rod out of the rod holder, remove the bells from the end of the rod (which brings the kids running again), then lovingly lean my fishing rod against the side of the camper. I ask the missus to grab me a fresh beer and I tell her how beautiful she looks in the bush. If I play my cards right, this could be one of the best days of my life.

FISHING TIPS AND TALES

TIPS FOR CATCHING YELLOW BELLY

- Use a 15kg breaking strain line.

- Use 4 to 6/0 hook. Yellow belly have huge mouths.

- Where possible, use fresh yabbies.

- Fish in the early morning and with the setting sun.

- Watch out for pelicans – they're fishing just like you.

- Fillet your fish, dip it in flour and cook it on the barbeque.

THE FISHING TRIP

FISHING KNOTS AND TIES

Knowing how to tie knots is an all-important part of a successful fishing experience. Tying good knots ensures that your equipment provides a tempting lure to fish and not a great mess that scares them off. It ensures you will not lose that prize catch when you haul it aboard. And it will also make it easier to change hook size, sinker size, etc, without a lot of mucking around.

12 OF THE BEST

The following 'Twelve Apostles' knots are considered essential tools for every angler. (Also check out the many instructional fishing videos that include sections on knot tying.)

FISHING TIPS AND TALES

Line to terminal tackle

    1. Locked half blood knot

    2. Paloma knot

    3. Uni knot

Loops

    4. Tagless dropper

    5. Perfection loop

    6. Twisted dropper loop

Braid lines

    7. Braid leader knot

    8. Braid ring knot

Joining lines

9. Double uni knot

10. Four-fold blood knot

Double knots

11. Plaited double

12. Bimini twist

There are hundreds of knots but the above 12 are sufficient for all but the most highly specialised angler. Here is how they are tied:

LINE TO TERMINAL TACKLE

1. LOCKED HALF BLOOD KNOT

This is a simple yet strong knot suitable for tying hooks and swivels to your line. It's a great one when you're after whiting or snapper.

FISHING TIPS AND TALES

1. Thread the eye of your hook or swivel and twist the tag and main line together.

2. Twist this three to six times and thread it back through the first twist. Choose fewer twists for a heavier line.

3. Pull the line so the knot begins to form, but not all the way just yet.

4. To lock it, thread the tag through the open loop that has formed at the top of the knot.

5. Pull the knot up firmly and you have yourself a locked half blood.

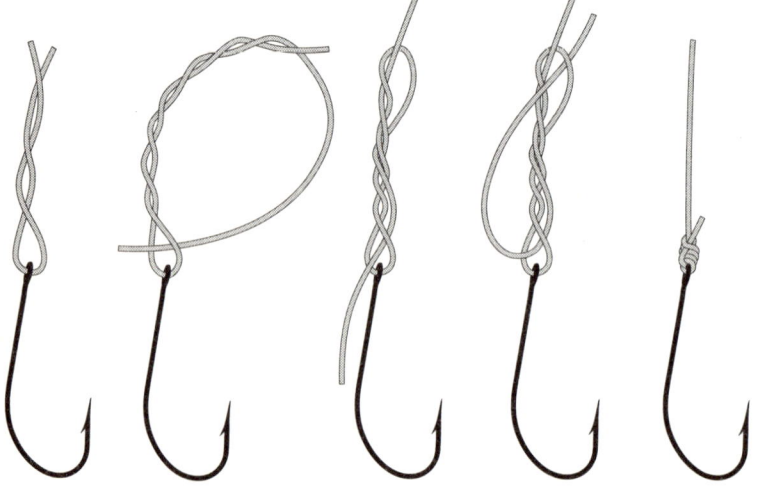

THE FISHING TRIP

Tip: If you end up with a bit of a loop in your knot, just pull on the tag until it disappears.

2. PALOMA KNOT

This knot is considered one of the strongest knots, even though it is actually quite simple. In fact, you can tie this knot at night or when you've had just one too many.

1. Double about 12.5cm of line and pass it through the eye of your hook.

2. Tie a simple overhand knot in the doubled line.

3. Leave the hook to hang loose.

4. Pull the end of loop down, passing it completely over the hook.

5. Pull both ends of the line to draw up the knot.

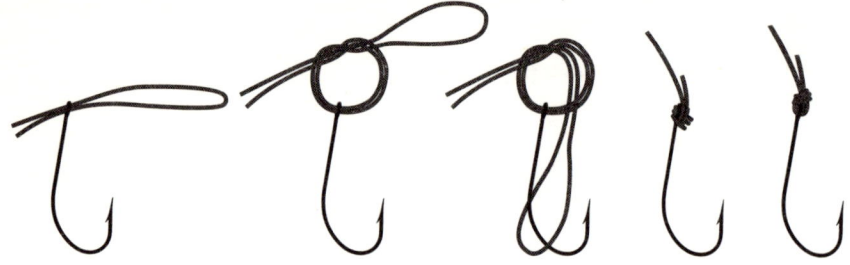

Tip: Make sure you don't twist the lines.

3. UNI KNOT

The uni knot is suitable for attaching lures, hooks and swivels.

   1. Pass the line through the eye of the hook and bring the tag back around to form a loop.

   2. Wrap the tag back around the line 3 to 5 times.

   3. Pass the tag through the loop.

THE FISHING TRIP

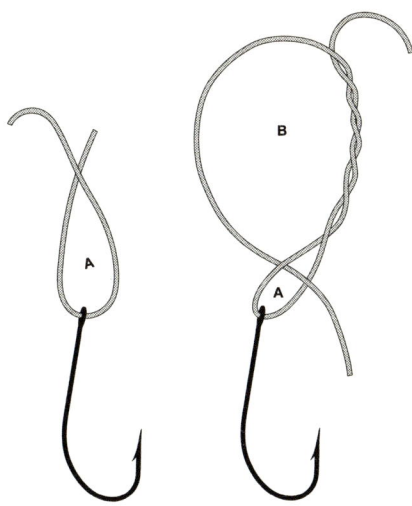

4. Repeat the above procedure with the tag until it ends up protruding from loop B alongside the main line.

5. Form the knot by pulling the tag against loop A.

6. Slide the knot down onto the hook.

FISHING TIPS AND TALES

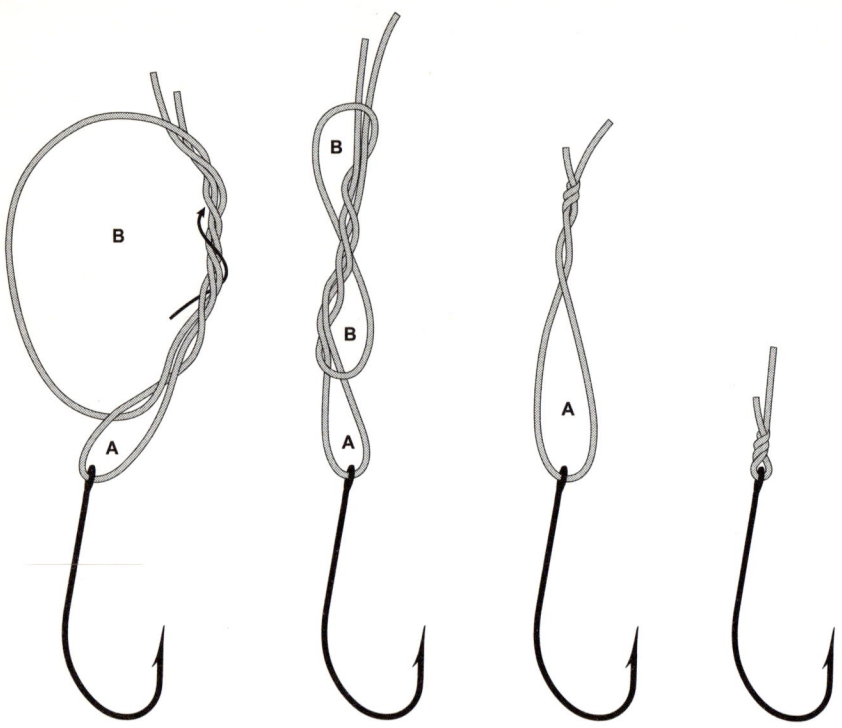

Tip: Some twists may remain in loop A, but that's cool.

LOOPS

4. TAGLESS DROPPER

This loop can be tied anywhere along your line, which means you can use as many as you like. It is a stronger

THE FISHING TRIP

and therefore better option to the standard figure eight.

1. Make a circle or loop in the line.

2. Insert a matchstick to one side of the crossover.

3. Rotate the match to put a twist in the line. Repeat this until there are three to four twists.

4. Remove the match, making sure you don't lose your place, and pull the doubled section of your loop through.

5. Pull the knot tight. Don't panic when the sequences reverse so that the loop is feeding from the centre of the knot. This is exactly what you want.

6. The finished knot should look like this (see illustration).

FISHING TIPS AND TALES

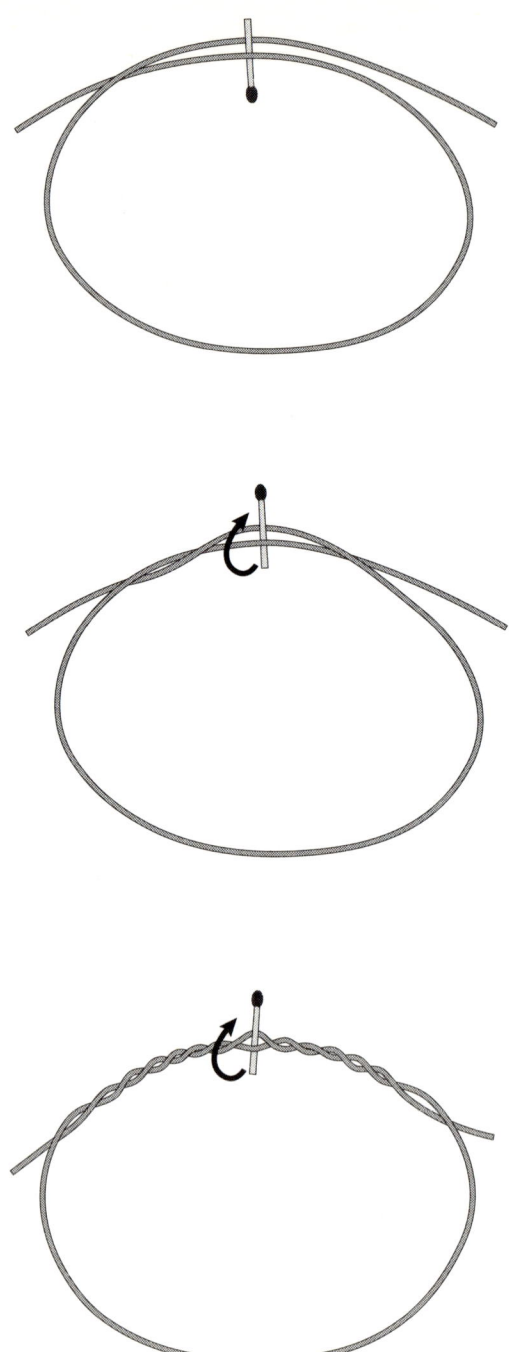

124

THE FISHING TRIP

5. PERFECTION LOOP

This is a dependable and strong loop when formed properly. You can use it to connect lures or flies to a

FISHING TIPS AND TALES

heavy leader or trace. It is one of the better loops because it will not kill the action of the lure or fly.

1. Take the line and form a loop by crossing the tag end over itself.

2. Leave about 10cm of the tag end exposed to work with.

3. Bring the tag end in front of the first loop to form a smaller loop in front of the larger loop.

4. Take the tag end; wrap it around the back of both loops and then between the two loops.

5. Reach through the first formed loop and take the second smaller loop and pull it through the first loop.

6. Slowly pull on the standing line while continuing to hold the smaller loop that you have pulled through.

THE FISHING TRIP

7. Trim the tag end close and the loop knot is complete.

Tip: It is useful to moisten the lines when you tie a knot.

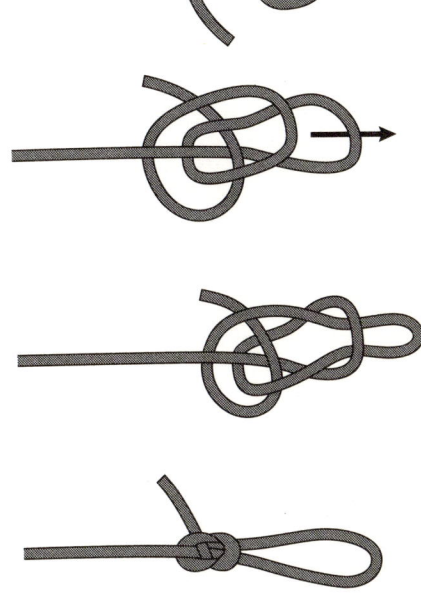

6. TWISTED DROPPER LOOP

Twisted lines are always a pain the butt. The twisted dropper loop can be used to attach a hook at any point along the line so that it is most unlikely to tangle. It is also ideal to use as a replacement for a three-way swivel.

1. Twist your line so that a twisted loop is formed.

2. Twist your line to extend your loop to the length required.

3. Cross the lines to form an open loop and insert your finger at the crossover so that the loop remains open.

4. Twist the crossing lines together, making four complete twists, or eight half twists.

5. Remove your finger and thread the twisted loop through at the crossover.

6. Close the knot up tight by pulling on both sides of the knot.

7. Thread your hook on shown.

THE FISHING TRIP

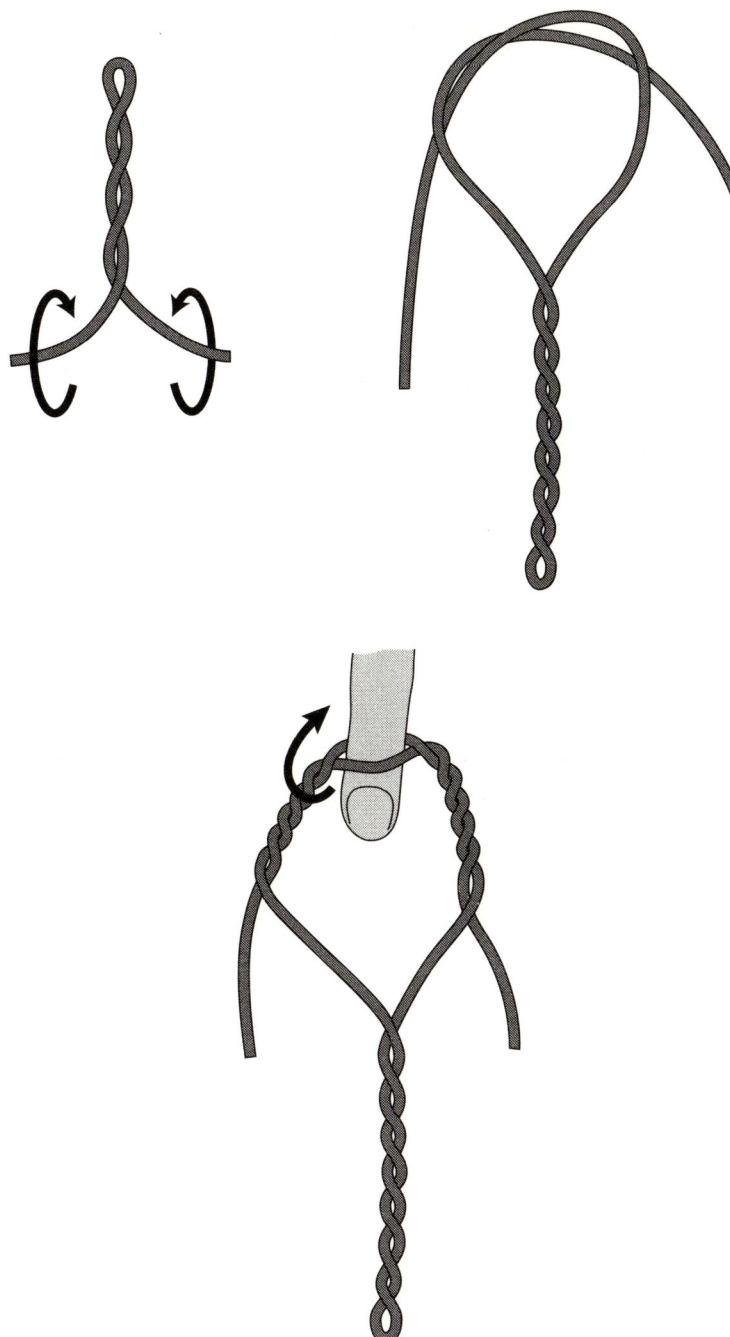

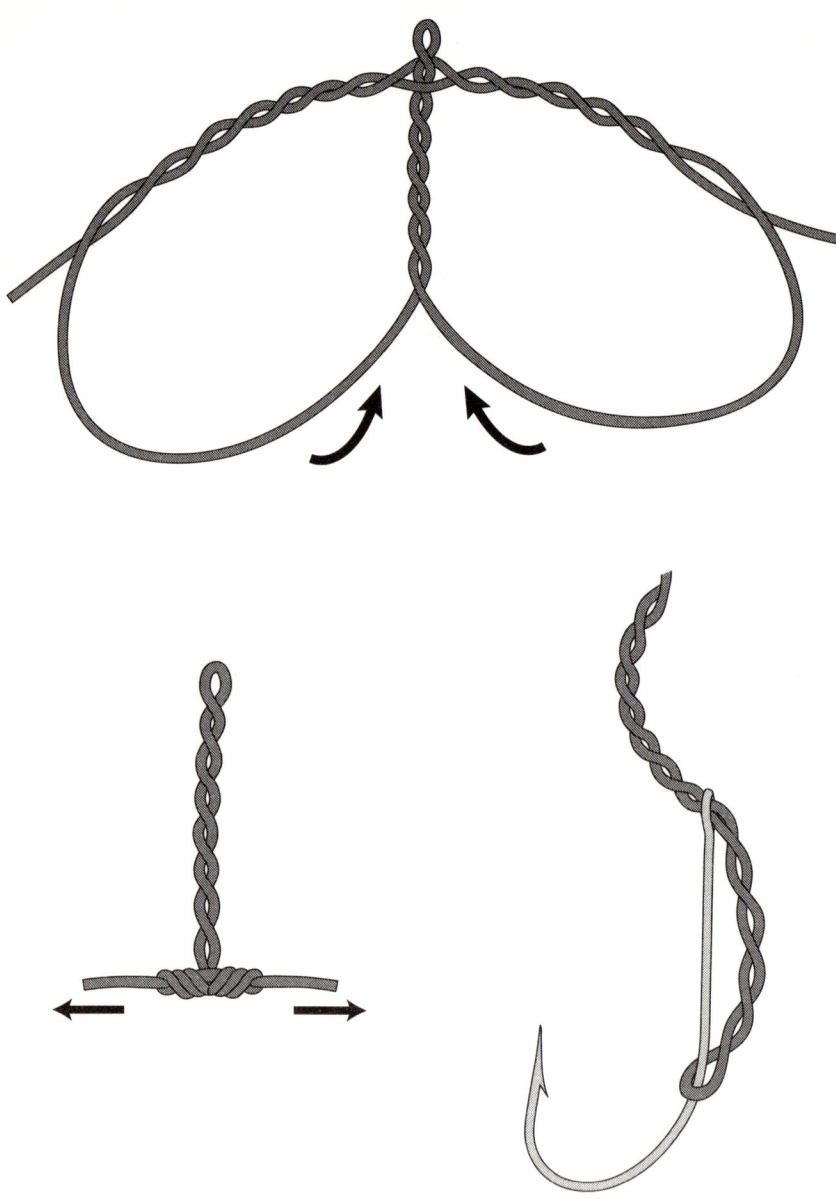

Tip: The twisted dropper now stands clear of the main line and will prevent line tangle.

THE FISHING TRIP

BRAID LINES

7. BRAID LEADER KNOT

This is the strongest way to tie a single strand of gelspun line to a monofilament leader.

1. Wind the gelspun line (illustrated in black) around one end of the monofilament leader about 20 times.

2. Tie a knot in the twisted lines and pull the monofilament leader through.

3. Repeat this to make another wrap.

4. Repeat another two times so there are four wraps.

5. Take hold of all four ends and close the knot with a firm but gentle pressure.

6. Close the knot firmly and trim the tags.

FISHING TIPS AND TALES

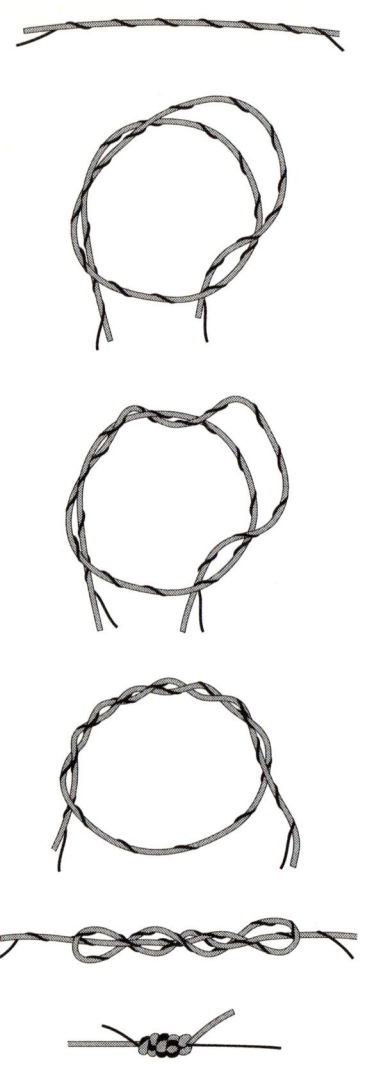

Tip: If a loop of slack gelspun appears, release the mono leader tag and apply pressure to the gelspun until it disappears.

8. BRAID RING KNOT

This is simply a blood knot with two wraps around the eye of the hook and quite a few more twists thrown in.

THE FISHING TRIP

1. Pass the line twice through the eye of the hook leaving plenty of tag.

2. Wind the tag around the main line five or six times.

3. Then wind it back again the same number of times.

4. Thread the tag through the centre of both ring wraps.

5. Slide the knot closed with gentle pressure on the main line.

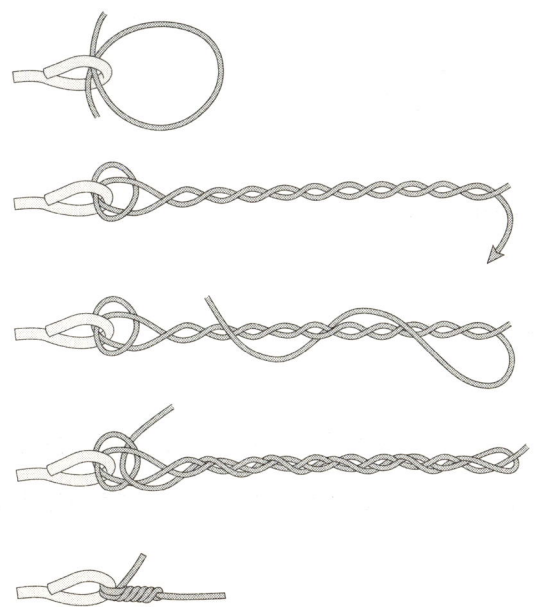

Tip: You may need to gently push the knot back as you go to keep the twists in place.

JOINING KNOTS

9. DOUBLE UNI KNOT

This is one of those knots that you really must know. It is used to join lines together whether they are the same or different.

1. Overlap the lines to be joined and encircle one line with the tag of the other.

2. Wrap the double strand inside this loop.

3. Make four wraps in total.

4. Close the knot, but don't tighten, and repeat with the other length of line.

5. Two knots should now be formed, one in each line, around each other.

6. Slide the knots together. Tighten and trim the tags.

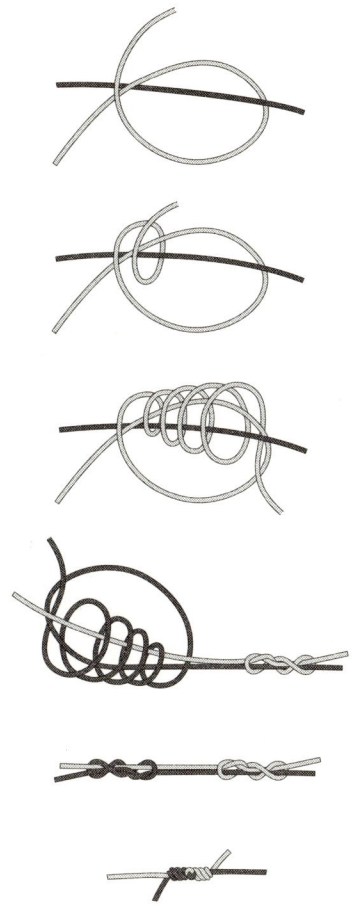

10. FOUR-FOLD BLOOD KNOT

This is a good knot because it is neat, easy, and still quite strong. It is best used to join two lines of the same or similar diameters.

1. Overlap the two lines.

2. Twist both ends together.

3. Repeat eight or nine times.

4. Pass each tag through the central twist from the opposite direction.

5. Close the knot carefully, putting tension on each side of the line.

6. Close the knot tightly and trim the tags.

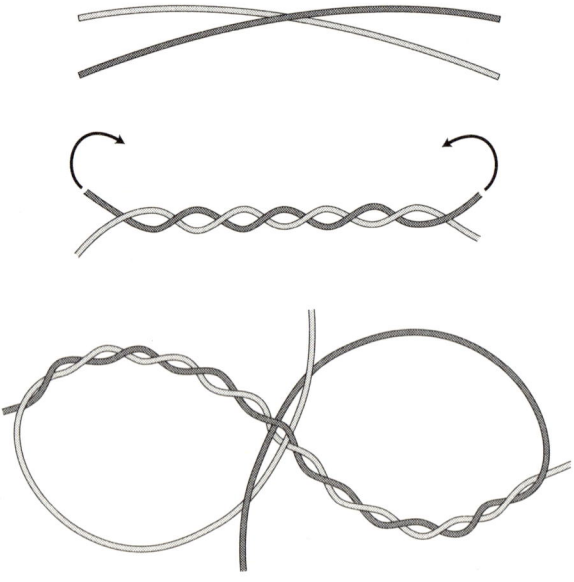

THE FISHING TRIP

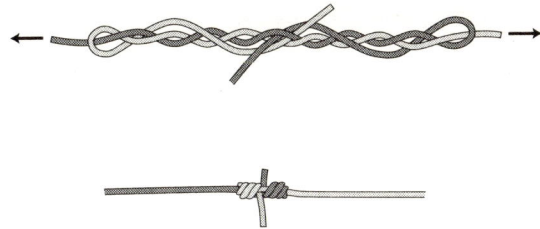

DOUBLE KNOTS

11. PLAITED DOUBLE

1. Measure off twice the length of line your finished double will be.

2. The main line is A. The returning length is B, and the tag is C.

3. Let's call the loop formed, D.

4. Keep the line tight and pass C over B (alongside A).

5. Pull B tight and maintain tension throughout the plaiting process.

6. Pass B over A and pull A tight.

7. Pass C over B and pull C tight.

8. This is the complete cycle of the plait. Keep the tension on the line. Some distortion may appear at the beginning of the plait; this is normal.

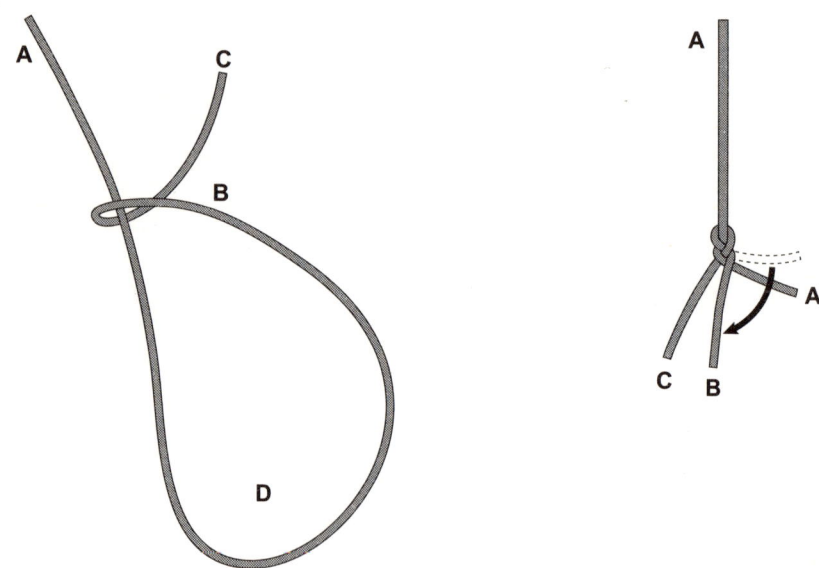

9. Plait for at least a dozen cycles and then double the tag over to form loop E as shown.

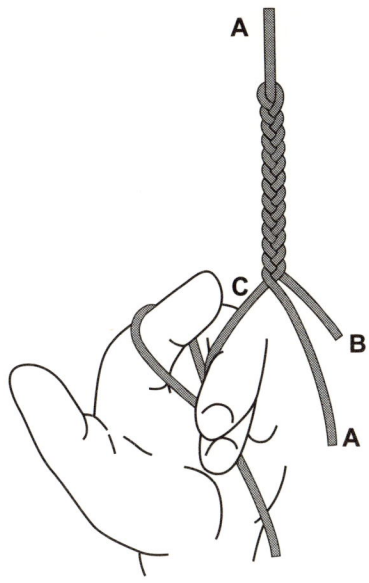

10. Loop E is plaited in just like the other two single legs. Secure the loop against the plait with the thumb and forefinger of the right hand as shown.

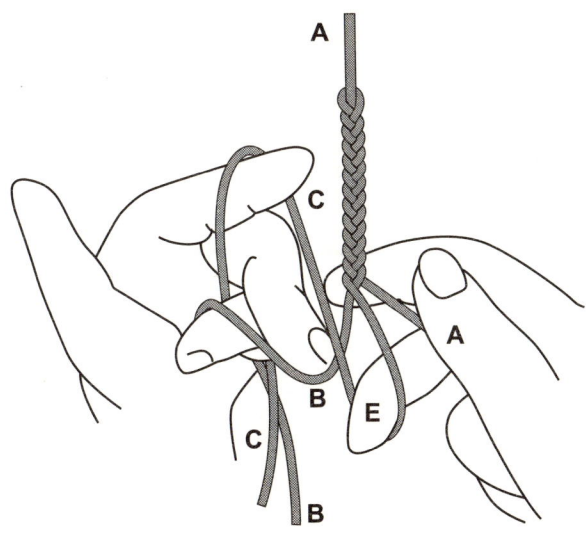

11. Transfer loop E to the index finger of your left hand and cross length B over it to the centre. Now pull E tight.

12. Continue to plait until you have a complete cycle. Then pass loop D through loop E.

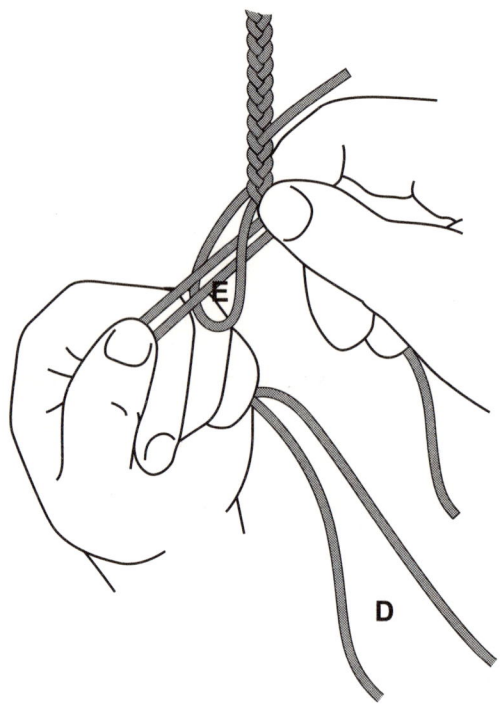

13. Pull the entire double through, by pulling on loop D against tag C to form a collar around the double.

THE FISHING TRIP

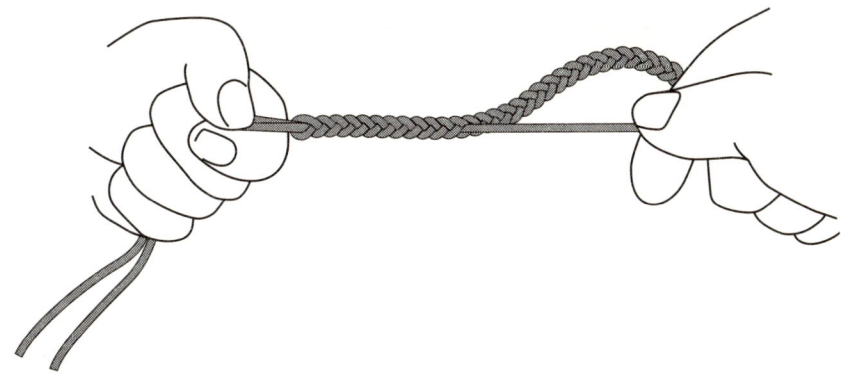

12. BIMINI TWIST

A bimini twist creates a long loop of line that is stronger than the line itself. A bimini twist is a simple method of doubling your fishing line in order to prevent chafing or to create the necessary loop in order to attach a wind-on leader. A short bimini twist (up to five feet) can easily be accomplished by one person. To tie a bimini twist longer than five feet takes two people, although it could be done alone with a lot of practice.

   1. Measure a little more than twice the length you will want for the double-line and sit down on a chair.

2. Run the line under your shoes and up to your thighs. Take the tag end in one hand and the rod end in the other. Hold both pieces of line in front of you and above your lap. You should feel like you are about to tie your legs and feet together.

3. With your knees together, twist the tag end of the line around the rod end about 10 or 12 times. You should now have a loop of line that goes under your shoes and is around both of your thighs, and closes at the twists above your lap.

4. Take the tag end of the line in one hand, the rod end in the other, and simultaneously begin moving your knees apart as you move your arms apart. This will shorten and tighten the twists in the line in front of you.

THE FISHING TRIP

5. Continue this until the twists are extremely tight.

6. Now begin to relax the tension on the hand that has the tag end. As you do so, continue the tension with your other arm and knees. Move the arm with the tag end down as the tension is released. The line will double back on itself and twist the other direction and down over the previous twists.

7. Continue tension and tie two half hitches around one of the single lines at the bottom of the twist.

8. Finish with two half hitches at the bottom of the twist around both lines.

FISHING TIPS AND TALES

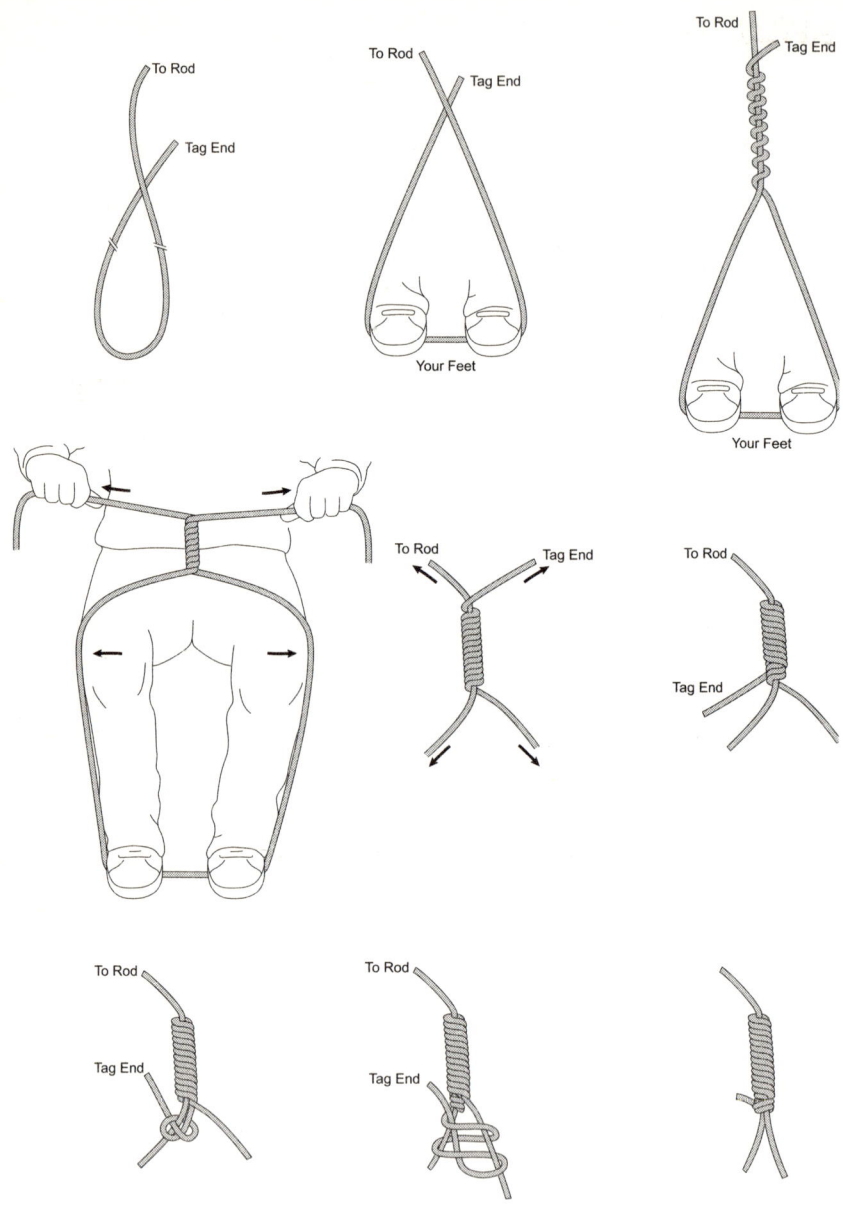

144

KNOT TIPS

- Knots in nylon should be moistened before pulling them tight. The best and quickest way is with saliva.

- Check and retie all knots after landing a large fish.

- Super glue can be used to finish off special knots such as bimini twists and braid knots.

- A 2cm piece of valve rubber makes an excellent cheap adjustable sinker stopper and reduces re-rigging time after tackle loss on snags.

BUYING A BOAT

We've all experienced boat fishing, whether it's been on a hired dinghy or courtesy of an invite from a wealthier friend (the best sort to have). Everyone is tempted at some stage to get a boat because, let's face it, you generally catch something from a boat. But which boat to buy? Before you make a costly investment, it's imperative to look at exactly what you *want* from a boat, what you *need* from a boat, and then be very honest about how much you'll *use* the boat.

Some questions for consideration:

- What sort of fishing do I want the boat for?

- Do I need to consider other uses, eg, family outings?

THE FISHING TRIP

- How many people do I need to carry?

- What size boat can I comfortably handle?

- Will I need to launch it alone?

- Is my vehicle capable of towing the boat and trailer I have my eye on?

- What size motor should I choose?

- Can I afford the boat I want now?

- Should I start out smaller?

- Can I afford all the expenses involved with owning a boat?

- Does my family share my enthusiasm?

These are all valid questions and if you don't ask them I'm sure your partner will. So be realistic. Remember, the second-hand boat you buy might be for sale because someone didn't bother asking these questions – or didn't answer them honestly.

CAR TOPPERS

A car topper is generally between 3m and 4m, making it suitable to be carried on the top of your vehicle. The seller may claim you can manage it yourself but, in reality, removing this size boat from the roof of a car on your own will be difficult. To make the task easier, fit your roof with special rollers.

TRAILER BOATS

If you want to invest in a decent boat there is a huge range available, from flat bottoms to V hulls, centre console to rear mounts, inboard or outboard, with a canopy or without. It's a matter of looking around and deciding what you want in a boat and factoring in the type of waters you want to fish.

THE FISHING TRIP

TIPS

- If you intend doing a lot of river fishing choose a flat-bottomed boat.

- Got fair skin? Make sure you get a canopy.

- After something that can pull a water skier? Make sure your motor has the power.

- Take your time and go to a reputable dealer.

- Make sure you can get after-sales service.

FISHING TIPS AND TALES

THE ABORTED FISHING TRIP

Fishing is not restricted to any particular age group or gender. Its appeal is universal and it's relatively inexpensive and lots of fun. As with many things, sometimes the preparations leading up to the event are bigger than the event itself.

A few years ago, my mates and I were tired of doing nothing, week in week out. So we decided to go on a no-expenses-spared fishing trip. We booked a 12 foot aluminium dinghy to go fishing for flathead, or flatties, off McCrea in Victoria. It would clearly be the highlight of our social calendar.

We planned to depart at 5.30 on Sunday morning, but we were in a quandary. Why go to bed a midnight and rise just four hours later. Instead, we decided to stay up all night and go fishing very early. But what to do until 4am?

THE FISHING TRIP

We kicked off around 8pm with a footy match on the television. It was going to be one of those multidiscipline sports weekends, anyone could tell. We gave it our best during the game in the time-honoured tradition of sport enthusiasts, everyone doing their bit and finishing their allotted beverages.

At 10.30pm someone suggested we just have an early night, so we cracked open a bottle of tequila and brought out the cards. At midnight, and two all, the game was abandoned. Too many cards had been sucked on and there were lemons in the middle of the table.

We switched on the television and the kettle. An early morning news bulletin included a warning about the weather, but it seemed irrelevant.

At 2am there's dissension in the group: two out of four want to go to bed. The weather report comes on again. There's a wind warning for the bay. What bay? Wind? Hardly worth listening to. One goes to bed; the remaining fishermen feel smug at their endurance.

FISHING TIPS AND TALES

At 2.30am the weather report indicates gusty wind on the bay.

The 3am wether bulletin mentions the word 'blue', which we interpret as the colour of the sky. Feeling optimistic, we get out the fishing boxes and begin to check tackle and hooks.

At 4am, we're listening to the weather report as we drive down the Frankston Flinders Road. Blue alert: not safe for small fishing craft. What do they know, we ask, and continue to drive.

The drive to McCrea is slow. The wind is nearly pushing our little two-door off the road. Halfway there it starts to rain, but we all know a little bit of rain never hurt anyone.

When we arrive in McCrea it's teeming with rain and almost impossible to find the landmark for the boat hire. We turn on the radio again to hear more news about blue alerts.

THE FISHING TRIP

We find the dinghies and our spirits soar; they wouldn't be out unless it was okay to use them. We pretend we had no doubt as we drive in. The girls stay in the car because it's still pelting down. By the time the boys return, the windows are completely fogged over and there's not much sign of life. The boys deliver the bad news: there'll be no fishing today.

We drive home slowly. The road conditions are horrible. We crawl into bed at 6am and swear we'll go fishing next weekend.

TIPS FOR FLATHEAD FISHING

When someone asks, 'What did ya catch?', how often do you hear the answer: 'Flathead'?

Flathead is the universal catch — the one we all love to hook. Here's some tips on catching it.

- Flathead are obliging fish: they respond to all methods of angling.

- Troll at slow speeds along the edges of banks and drop-offs. Use hard-bodied bibbed lures and soft plastics.

- All types of lures work well, including flies. A jerky slow retrieve works best.

- Use dead and live baits along the edges of weed beds, banks and reefs.

- Large flathead are caught on surf beaches on poppers and baits.

THE FISHING TRIP

- In estuaries, flathead holding areas can be detected at low tide by finding indentations of flathead shapes in the soft sand.

FISHING TIPS AND TALES

THE FAMILY OUTING

Deciding to take the entire family fishing is just plain stupid. How can four to six members of one family enjoy doing the same thing? It probably means you won't catch anything all day, not to mention the other hazards.

- What will you do when your kids keep throwing bait at each other?

- What will you say when your youngest wants to know if the dead fish will go straight to heaven?

- How can enjoy it if your eldest keeps asking, 'When are we going home?'

THE FISHING TRIP

- How will you cope when your wife says, 'Of course we're not going to eat them', and asks you to remove the hook from your prize catch and let it swim away.

It's best to discourage whole-family fishing expeditions. Instead, break them down into age groups or gender, or simply fish with those who want to fish. Movies are great for those who aren't interested. If the entire family *wants* to go fishing, all you can do is grin and bear it, and try some of these suggestions.

TIPS FOR FISHING WITH KIDS

- Keep sessions short and interesting. Waiting hours for snapper is just pure boredom for a child.

- Hand lines are the simplest form of fishing and an ideal way to introduce children to the excitement of fishing.

FISHING TIPS AND TALES

- Wait for optimum conditions. Cold, wet kids usually don't enjoy themselves.

- Give children all the help they need with their rods. Don't compete with them this early in their angling lives.

- At the first signs of seasickness, take the kids back to shore and try again another day.

- Explain why undersized fish are returned and let the kids release the fish themselves.

- Always have adequate toilet facilities available.

- You're after a lifetime companion. Praise is the way to go for even the most humble efforts.

- Try to photograph the first catch and any notable catches thereafter for the family album.

- Make sure you have a few tasty snacks and drinks.

THE FISHING TRIP

- Avoid the blood and gore part of fishing. Dispose of or clean fish as humanely as possible.

- The worst gift to give a junior or novice angler is cheap tackle. The inevitable malfunction will be discouraging and frustrating.

- Joining an angling club – many offer reduce membership fees for families.

- Above all, have fun. Keep the humour and goodwill flowing for the whole trip and remember that fishing is a grand adventure for any child.

TROUT FISHING

I have always thought of trout fishing as the dignified arm of angling. There's nothing better than a couple of close mates, pristine rivers and a peaceful day or so away. And what better reward for your dedication than a fair fight for your fish, the simple pleasure of stuffed trout, followed by a good port by an open fire?

Yet we all know that catching trout can be frustrating. Perhaps some of these tips will help make your next adventure more productive.

- The nymph stage of the dragonfly is called a mudeye by anglers. Mudeyes are probably the best trout bait of all. Dragging a hand-held shrimp net amongst reeds in permanent water ponds can collect them. They should be kept in water. If allowed to dry out they quickly

THE FISHING TRIP

become dragonflies, the next stage in its life cycle.

- In deep lakes, lightly weighted bait dropped straight down below the boat can often produce action. Brown trout in particular are quite at home in such deep water.

- Fine rubber bands may be used to secure baits such as grasshoppers, crickets and cicadas to the hook.

- A wire coat hanger can be easily bent to make a rod rest when fishing on riverbanks.

- Fish are sensitive to vibrations and the shallower the water the more likely your noise will startle them.

- Lead core lines can be purchased for trolling. Their colour changes over their length with each colour said to lower the lure 1m as the line is paid out. A wide centre pin reel and a

FISHING TIPS AND TALES

stiff rod are the most suitable for hard-core lines.

- In times of flood, trout and other fish leave the streams and forage where the land was once dry. Local farmers and residents will often take advantage of this and catch large fish in their own paddocks.

- Some of the best trout fishing pools occur below waterfalls in highland streams.

- When trolling for trout a very slow speed is required. On some impoundments a fish box is towed on ropes in the outboard wash to slow the boat to walking pace.

- Trout anglers often observe a stretch of water for some time before attempting to fish. Using Polaroids they try to spot and mark individual fish or likely places where fish might inhabit.

THE FISHING TRIP

- Brown trout are very hard to catch in broad daylight. Fishing in the last hour of daylight can produce excellent results.

- Jungle green is said to be the best colour to wear when stalking fish in clear streams.

- When fishing lakes and rivers with heavy weed growth, sinkers and baits are hidden from the fish. Where weed growth prevents normal fishing, trying casting a small bubble float or weighted float with suspended bait over the weed bed.

- Saltwater mussels make excellent bait for trout.

- Farmers sometimes deny anglers access to their land because they break off branches for campfires and leave bait bags and rubbish by the banks of streams. Always carry out your rubbish and use small dead wood, preferably collected well away from the banks, for your campfires.

FISHING TIPS AND TALES

- Fly fishermen and others who wade streams and rivers try to do so unencumbered by backpacks, creels and tackle boxes. They wear special vests with many pockets and attach lures and flies to their hats.

- 'Cow bells' and 'Ford Fenders' are flashers used to attract trout. They are trolled at slow speeds ahead of a lure or bait. Rigging instructions come with each flasher.

TROUT FARMS

Never had any luck catching trout? Consider visiting a trout farm. It's a great day out for all the family. Just remember to take a picnic lunch to offset some of the costs.

At a trout farm you purchase bait, which resembles wet rolled up chicken feed, and are supplied with a fishing rod. There are usually several channels containing trout of various sizes. Establish where the

THE FISHING TRIP

smaller fish are kept and point your children in that direction.

At the end of the excursion your fish must be passed in and weighed. You will be charged a set price per kilogram for the fish you have caught. If each family member catches one decent trout, this can be quite costly. If you decide this is the best (easiest) fishing you've ever done and don't know when to stop, you'll end up spending a small fortune. We recommend that you let the kids catch the fish while you watch, assist and encourage. And stay away from the channel that holds the big mother fish!

FISHING WITH WOMEN

Every now and then a man gets tempted to invite his girlfriend/wife fishing. Fishing is something you love and if she enjoyed it too, wouldn't life be perfect? Well you can try fishing with women, but be prepared. Here's some tips.

TIPS FOR MEN

Some women love to fish. It's a great pastime. But let's not forget that women are different to men and, quite simply, they have different priorities. A man wants a full esky, a couple of mates and a fish at the end of the day. Women, however, like to be comfortable. There is no such thing as 'making do'. Why sit on the cold, hard ground when you can sit in a chair? Why eat soggy sandwiches when you can dine

THE FISHING TRIP

on chicken and champagne? Just because you're roughing it, there's no need to be feral.

TIPS FOR WOMEN

Quality time with your man can be hard to come by. You're both always so busy with careers, footy, cricket and the kids that it's a wonder you get *any* time alone. So when he invites you fishing, don't respond with 'I'd rather visit an old people's home'. Think outside the square. A fishing trip is great fun and can be modified to suit your own needs.

ADVICE FOR SUN LOVERS

Only consider invitations to fish from a boat. Do not be elitist – a small dinghy will do – but if you are in a position to be choosy, a larger craft is more comfortable and you'll be less inclined to feel the need to fish. (They are fitted with a lounge.)

Fishing is great way to work on your tan. You are exposed to the sun for several hours, you benefit from the reflection off the water, and there's no need to move around much. Perfect conditions. If you set off early, which unfortunately is preferable if you want to catch fish, you'll get a good six hours on the boat. Expose your body gradually as the morning warms up and apply sunscreen at regular intervals. Don't forget a hat. You'll need it for comfort and practicality. (When you're back on land, you can freshen up while he cleans the fish.)

During the day, try fishing. I know this may seem extreme and you will get fish smelling hands, but how's this for motivation – it makes you move just enough to expose those parts of the body to the sun that sometimes miss out from 'regular' sunbathing.

Did I mention catching fish is actually great fun? But a word of warning: don't get too competitive. Men like to catch the biggest fish; men don't expect you to enjoy gutting fish; and men like to see you squirm when they swing the oozy black squid in your face. Remember these simple rules and you should both enjoy the outing.

THE FISHING TRIP

ADVICE FOR CAREER WOMEN

If you decide to go fishing, don't sulk, and don't discuss the ecological and animal cruelty aspects of fishing. Focus your energies on choosing a suitable fishing destination. Perhaps a tranquil lake or a deserted stretch of beach. Maybe somewhere that has toilets or hot coffee. Do your homework, or have your personal assistant do the research for you.

Take a comfortable chair, a rug and plenty of good food and wine. The most important thing to remember is that just because you're not in the office, it doesn't mean that you can't get some work done. Allow yourself a 10-minute break every hour to look at the scenery.

Not surprisingly, you'll find that fishing spots are the perfect location for work. There's no-one around to interrupt you and the last thing your partner will want to do is chat; he's after a fish.

During the day you may be tempted to try fishing. Be warned: it's addictive. Once you get that first little bite and you wind in your line to realise that the bait is gone, you may feel the competitive need to catch whatever it is that's down there. If the worst thing that happens is you actually unwind and relax for half an hour, will that really be so bad? And what if you actually catch a fish? As long as it's the correct size, what the hell; throw caution and principles to the wind and just keep it.

If you get caught up in the sheer fun of it all and realise you've been at it for 2 hours, don't panic – you can always look over those papers on the drive back home.

WHERE NOT TO TAKE WOMEN FISHING

Fishing from a bank usually requires a bit of a walk. If you want your female companion to be totally peeved by the time you arrive at the bank, park a long way away and make her carry half the gear. Alternatively, you can drive as close as possible to the destination, unpack the car, leave her there and go to find a suitable parking place, even if that's up to 1km away.

THE FISHING TRIP

Once you have returned and carried all the gear to the 'perfect spot' try not to become too agitated when she says, 'It looks better over there'. Move quickly and quietly and all should be well.

Make sure her chair is set up in her preferred position; shade if she has fair skin, full sun if she's a sun-worshipper. Make sure she can reach the esky and don't panic if she's removed all your cans to accommodate her avocado dip.

Remember to bait her hook and try not to complain when she casts right into the tree. Climb as far up the tree as you can and do your best to get the hook out of the bark. Cutting and re-doing the line might be easier.

When you've done the perfect cast and your line is drifting just into the shadows about two feet from the river gum that's grown out of the bank and is home to some of the best fish around, don't, I repeat don't, be upset when she decides to dip her feet in just for a minute. Of course the ripples probably mean a fish is escaping and the nibbled bait is going to drive you to the point of distraction, but remember – you invited her.

Come lunchtime, while she's distracted, get in a few good hours of fishing. Move down stream slightly, pretend you're deaf and enjoy.

Show no sign of anger when she remarks that she left her favourite jumper in the car and asks if you wouldn't mind grabbing it. Recognise this for what it truly is – an elaborate plan to cut the fishing trip short. Remember, in a couple of hours the sun will be on the way down and the fish will be out hunting for a nice juicy worm.

Above all else, do not believe her when she says crows attacked the bait container while you were gone. Give her the jumper, dig up some more worms, then move 100m down stream and fish until dark.

This may or may not be the end of your relationship, but when you're wiping the slime off your beautiful

THE FISHING TRIP

fish, when you're gutting and cleaning it, when your taking your own souvenir photo at home, take heart: at least you got one.

WHERE TO FISH

FISHING FROM BOATS

Fishing from a boat allows you to cover a larger part of a body of water than shore fishing. In their simplest form, boats can be nothing more than a platform that you sit or stand on. Some boats are made for rivers and streams, for small lakes, or for large bodies of water.

As the operator of a boat you are legally responsible for the boat and the safety of those on board. You must also understand the rules of navigation and the courtesies of safe boating.

If you decide to try fishing from a boat, there is a lot to know before you go. You need to know about:

- The boat and how it handles.

- The equipment on the boat and how it works.

- The waters you will be boating on and any hazards such as submerged trees and rocks.

- The weather conditions and emergency procedures.

- The safety devices on the boat and how they work.

- Your own personal abilities: how much you can do before you become too tired.

FISHING TIPS AND TALES

Here's some more tips and suggestions about fishing in boats:

BOATING SAFETY

- Before going angling in a boat always obtain the latest weather forecasts.

- Log your details with the coast guard: boat registration, description, number of passengers, destination and estimated time of arrival. Keep this information handy on a waterproof card, and don't forget to log off each day – overdue boats are subject to search and rescue.

- Attach a float to boat key rings.

- If you're launching a boat at a new location check for slippery surfaces, wave surge over the ramp and availability at low tide.

- Marine radios are essential. Note that a two-way conversation closes the particular channel to all other communication for the period of the conversation, so keep radio talks short.

- Bare feet have no place in any fishing boat. Dropped knives, fish spikes and teeth, hooks and heavy sinkers can cause serious injury.

- Most boat owners have GPS navigation aids. It is essential that GPS coordinates have a written back-up; if the instrument is damaged, lost or stolen the coordinates will be lost completely.

- If you do not have GPS instruments, rely on landmarks. The most accurate landmarks are taken with the boat at the point of a right-angled triangle. Two points are aligned on each side. It is more accurate to choose a near point, say a church spire, with a far point, say a hill, rather than have two points quite close together.

- Pieces of plastic tube threaded over the point of a gaff can prevent injuries on boats.

- When launching, make sure the car is in park and the handbrake is on. Some anglers add a wheel chock for additional insurance against launching the car as well.

- If you get caught in an electrical storm, lower the radio aerial, turn off all equipment including echo sounders and reduce the boat's profile by lowering all rods. Stay low in the middle of the boat or in the cabin until the danger has passed.

- Nylon and braid fishing line caught around boat propellers needs to be removed by raising the skeg and using whatever means necessary, even cutting. On return to shore, remove the propeller and check for any remaining line. Nylon and braid can damage seals and cause serious problems.

WHERE TO FISH

- When contemplating fishing any estuary by boat, inspect the area at low tide and co-relate what is observed with an accurate chart. This simple precaution avoids being stranded on sandbanks and helps to identify likely productive fishing areas.

ON THE WATER

- When anchored in a boat, always leave the motor in gear. Propellers spin slowly in the current or tide if the boat is in neutral thus tangling lines and causing potential damage to oil seals. Spare bungs should always be part of the emergency kit in every boat. A lost bung can be disabling in a remote location.

- When proceeding out of estuary entrances to oceans for the first time, it is wise to follow an experienced skipper. Mark a waypoint every 100m or so and then reverse them for the return journey. As conditions and visibility deteriorate, waypoints become essential to safety.

- Bridling a boat is a simple operation. This prevents a boat yawing on the end of the anchor rope. Tie a rope from the boat's stern to the anchor rope, making the boat the base of an equilateral triangle.

- Automatic berley dispensers can be purchased commercially. They look like an old-fashioned milk shake blender and they fit in the top of the berley pot. A lid can be made to fit any size berley pot from plastic or wood. Attach to a 12-volt battery and you have a no-hands operation. Refill the pot as needed.

- Recovering anchors over the side of the boat using the buoy system is safe and easy but it does scratch fibreglass and aluminium. A piece of old carpet or a heavy hessian bag kept near the recovery side can be unrolled and draped over the side when needed.

WHERE TO FISH

- While many boat crews share their fish catch evenly, others may wish to identify their own fish. Snipping tails and fins, individual keeper nets, buckets or bins and different coloured elastic bands can all be used to separate fish.

- When choosing a pump for an in-built or freestanding live-bait tank select the largest gallons per hour that is practical. The more through-put the more likely the bait will stay fresh and lively.

TROUBLE SHOOTING

- Failing a ladder, the best way to board a boat from the water is by way of the skeg of the outboard and the transom.

- Anchors sometimes get hooked on reefs and cannot be pulled free. The best way to free a steel anchor is to cleat the rope to the transom and let out at least 25m of rope. Then, keeping the tension on the rope, travel anticlockwise in a full circle. Usually this does the trick as at some point the anchor aligns with the hazard entry points.

- In still conditions, the damp surfaces of fibreglass boats attract sand flies like magnets. Use a brand name surface spray to solve the problem.

- Open aluminium boats can be noisy and adversely affect fishing in shallow water. Carpets, mats and even bags can be used to minimise noise on the boat floor.

- The speed of drifting can be reduced by trailing a sea-anchor or drogue behind the boat. A sea-anchor resembles a parachute and is very effective.

- The most thorough method of lure fishing from a boat is to progressively cast around an imaginary clock face or until the fish are located.

WHERE TO FISH

- Boat anglers are constantly wiping bait scraps, fish and salt from outboard motor covers. All companies making outboards now have covers available. These help protect the motor and increase resale value.

- By judicious use of berley, good numbers of fish can often be attracted right to the stern of the boat. Unfortunately, berley also attracts small fish and unsuitable species such as toadies. A long cast over the top of these small fish will often hook larger fish on the outskirts of the school.

ROCK FISHING

Rock fishing is the most hazardous form of angling and must be approached with respect and caution. Never go rock fishing alone, never turn your back on the ocean and always move around the rocks at a sensible pace. Always have an exit plan for if you are washed from the rocks. Look for a place where access to the land is possible, and lock it in your memory.

Here are some tips on rock fishing:

- Choose your footwear carefully. Light runners with ribbed soles and shoes or boots with raised edges help give a good grip on a slippery surface. Wearing waders, gumboots and thigh boots is inappropriate and dangerous.

WHERE TO FISH

- Long light rods are invaluable when rock fishing. One of the most productive ways to fish the stones is to use lightly weighted bait under a large float. This method is called bobby corking.

- Tie a rope around the tails of fish frames and let them wash in the surge. The scent and scraps will attract fish.

- The most productive areas to fish are turbulent patches of white water. Fish congregate here because the wave action dislodges food items from the rocks.

- Found attached to rocks, limpets and chitons are a cheap and readily available source of bait for many rock-fishing species such as drummer, bream and snapper.

- For high-speed spinning from rock platforms you'll need a long powerful rod (3.5m to 4.5m). Reels have a gear ratio of around 5:1

FISHING TIPS AND TALES

and are usually of a very high quality to take the stresses involved. Lures are torpedo shaped and weigh up to 150g.

- Secure balloons to floating bait presentations with lightweight elastic bands. Make a loop in the line and tie on the elastic. As the fish takes the bait the loop tightens, cutting the elastic, releasing the balloon and freeing the line for playing the fish.

- When live baiting for large fish from rocks or headlands it is wise to choose a location where the breeze will take the balloon or large float out to sea.

- A children's blow up wading pool makes an ideal storage pool for live bait. A bucket tied to a rope can be used to fill the pool.

- Lightweight tent poles can be screwed together to make a long cliff gaff.

FISHING THE BEACH

To beach or not to beach, that is the question. Fishing off the beach can certainly be frustrating and unproductive at first. But with a little knowledge and experience you'll be able to read a beach. You'll learn to spot the holes and gutters where the fish hang out, and you'll put your bait in the right place more often.

Check out these useful tips to give you an advantage over your marine adversaries:

- Landing a large fish on a surf beach requires patience. Try to get to the side of the fish and allow a wave to strand it. Or, keep the fish straight out to sea and wait for an appropriate wave to wash it in. Walk quickly back up the beach and hold the fish as the wave recedes.

FISHING TIPS AND TALES

Quick work is then required to reach the fish before the next wave.

- Sand crabs are a huge problem on many beaches. One way to keep bait longer in crab territory is to cut a groove in a cork or small piece of foam and half hitch it 10cm above the hook. The foam or cork may take a metre or two off the casting distance but it's worth the effort.

- Saltwater flies, cork surf-poppers and soft plastic lures can be used on paternoster and other surf fishing rigs in place of bait. Unlike natural baits these lures are sand-crab free.

- Belt bait-holders are a great idea – simply thread the belt through the container and fill it up. No more trekking back to the tackle cache.

- Surf fishing is probably the most weather-dependant form of angling. Many surf beaches are near estuaries so throw in a bream rod or

WHERE TO FISH

two when you going surf fishing and if the weather turns nasty it may not be necessary to return home after all.

- To sand-proof a surf reel that's not in use on the beach try knotting a shopping bag around and over the reel.

- Wise anglers cast and then walk with the current, increasing the time the baits are in the water. (Sometimes this method needs the cooperation of other anglers on the beach.)

- If you're striving for larger and longer casts from revolving or fixed spools, your sinkers and bottom rig may snap off during the cast. This is expensive, time wasting and dangerous: the sinker becomes a high-speed missile. The solution is to tie on 15m of heavy nylon to the main line to absorb the strain involved in distance casting.

FISHING TIPS AND TALES

- Some beaches have so called 'killer waves'. Keep your gear well up the beach and be alert for that big one that sweeps the beach.

- Bury your cold drinks and beverages in the sand to keep them cool. Mark the spot carefully with a stick or similar marker.

FISHING IN BAYS AND INLETS

Coastlines with bays and inlets can provide some of the most beautiful, exciting and productive fishing areas in the world. Here are some tips when you fish in these areas:

- On those wind-less, current-less days on estuaries, bays and inlets, remove sinkers altogether and allow the baits to fall naturally. It is surprising how many predatory fish will take unweighted bait.

- Fast currents in estuaries require special tactics. With a long trace to a stopper such as a split ring allow the current to take the bait to the required distance from the boat. Now attach a teardrop sinker to the line at the rod tip with a commercial product such as an Easy Rig or a split ring. The sinker slides along the line to the trace stopper slowly pulling the line and bait to where the fish are on the bottom.

- When fishing a fast current it is essential that the bait does not spin and twist the line. A few minute's extra care and a water test can avoid 50m of tangle.

- If you constantly lose baits such as sandworms, pipis and mussels to smaller fish, change to harder bait. Squid strips, unshelled prawns, small crabs, or small fish fillets may result in a larger fish.

- Tuna oil and poultry layer pellets make excellent berley for a variety of fish species. Use the raw pellets mixed with oil and scatter them on the water or make firm 'hand grenades' by mixing with water.

- Be prepared for fish to approach you.

GAME FISHING

Game fishing is for the serious angler who has a few dollars to spare. Here are some tips.

TAGGING

- The most important information on a tag is the tag number. This is the key to identifying the fish. It is critical to record the exact tag number.

- If you plan on releasing the fish, quickly write down the tag number, measure or estimate the fish's length, then gently release the fish with the tag in place. Multiple recaptures of tagged fish are particularly valuable to the tagging program.

FISHING TIPS AND TALES

- Tagging is an example of responsible and progressive attitude of anglers to the use of fisheries resources.

- Tables in journals show reasonably accurately a weight for length ratio. You can then estimate the weight of your catch before tagging or releasing the fish.

- Only affiliated members of registered game-fishing clubs can obtain tags.

TACKLE

- Stand-up game-fishing tackle includes shoulder harnesses, rod belts and buttock braces. They are invaluable in a long drawn out fight with a game fish.

- For game-fishing trolling, soft plastic lures in sizes over 15cm come in a variety of shapes and colours.

WHERE TO FISH

- Game anglers refer to fish-attracting devices as 'teasers'. There are many commercial products sold that rely on flash, splash and action to attract large fish such as marlin. Daisy chains of large plastic hook-less lures can also be used.

- Some game fishermen use small wide elastic bands to attach their live slimy mackerel baits to a hook for trolling. A piece of wire is bent like a crochet hook. The wire is pushed through the upper jaw of the bait and the loop of elastic is pulled through. The bottom half of the elastic is then placed over the top jaw and behind the top loop and tightened. The protruding loop is then attached to the hook with a double loop. Try it with a dead fish first. It is easy, effective and, unlike other forms of bait, bridling is said to be harmless.

- Small electrical cable ties are excellent for keeping hooks and lines in position on large live baits such as striped tuna.

FISHING TIPS AND TALES

- Anglers go to extreme lengths to release marlin unharmed. They use an instrument called a 'snooter', which is a stainless steel retractable bill rope on a stainless steel pole. It's placed over the bill to allows safe handling during de-hooking and tagging.

- A scoop net can be used to catch baitfish at night by the light of a strong torch or underwater light. Garfish, anchovies and pilchards appear to be dazzled and may be scooped up easily.

- Probably the greatest fishing lure of all time is the silver Wonder Wobbler. It dates back to the 1940s but is still going strong. They are now available in all colours and sizes, and the same magic wobble is still attracting fish.

- Specialised game-fishing tackle shops are located near main game fishing ports. Most have mail-order catalogues, which include the latest gear that may not be available in regular tackle shops.

ON THE BOAT

- Game fishermen in particular trail a berley slick behind their boats either at anchor or drifting. It is etiquette to pass to the bow of boats engaged in berleying as cutting the trail is said to scare off potential catches that may be following the trail to its source.

- Bomboras in the ocean are great places to fish. Observe the breaking seas before positioning your boat on the side. Keep the motor running for a quick getaway in case of a large roller crossing the rocks.

- Determine beforehand the order in which strikes are to be taken by anglers. For example, by an allotted time per angler, by a nominated angler to each rod or by taking it in turns on strikes. Frustrations arise when this is not clear to all on board.

- One of the most enduring angler superstitions concerns the humble banana. Many experienced skippers and charter boat operators refuse to have any bananas on board.

- Trolling with live baits requires the lowest possible boat speed. To reduce vibration the motor can be trimmed right up against the transom of the boat.

- The faster the trolling speed, the farther the lures should be from the boat.

- Noose large sharks in the first instance with a stainless steel wire noose with a rope attached. The rod is passed through the noose that is then fed over the shark's head and tightened around the body past the dorsal fin. Drive the boat away from the shark to tighten the noose. Tail nooses and ropes can be added.

- Fixed gaffes are very difficult to handle as the shark rolls. If you do want to gaff shark, the safest bet is to do so in the mouth.

WHERE TO FISH

- When tracing a marlin for gaffing keep the boat moving forward slowly. Stopping the boat allows the marlin to dive or sink.

- Charter boat operators have very sophisticated sounders that clearly show bait schools. The skippers maintain that where bait is found predators such as marlin, tuna and shark won't be far away.

- Do not neglect the prop wash as a place to troll a pelagic fish lure. The bubbles and foam created by the prop attract many fish such as marlin and tuna and this lure is quite often the first to be taken.

- Game fishermen know the value of water temperature gauges in their boat to detect warm currents.

PIER FISHING

Until recently I'd always been a bit suspicious of pier fishing. I'd rarely seen anyone catch very much off a pier. That was until I fished at Broome Pier in Western Australia.

It was the wet season when I visited, so there was limited access to fishing vessels (sensibly, they're in storage until the threat of cyclones has passed). Broome is a deep-water port and it caters to huge ships that move in and out of the waters, so the pier is massive. To give you an idea, it's big and strong enough to carry road trains. It is also extremely high. For those who don't like piers it is scary; for those who love them, it's a beauty.

In Broome there are tides anywhere from 3m to 10m twice daily. With these tides come hundreds of fish

WHERE TO FISH

and most of them head for the pier. At the correct time, an hour either side of the tide change, the pier becomes a supermarket with fish and anglers alike, looking for dinner.

To get some of the action, check your tidal charts. A good way to fail is to turn up at the pier at a time that bears no relation to whether the fish are around or indeed hungry. If the fish aren't biting, you won't catch one. It's that simple.

Once I'd sorted out the tides, I knew we were in for a great week's fishing. For the first two days we went through the usual motions: cast, open a beer, sit back and relax. But on this trip, the water became too active to ignore. An hour after the change of low tide the activity would start. First we'd see some movement in the water; a large 'cloud' that appeared to be moving. These clouds were large schools of baitfish. Shortly after, fish would dive out of this mass sending baitfish in every direction. As we kept watching, these fish were pursued by even larger fish.

FISHING TIPS AND TALES

Once these large fish made it to the pylons of the pier we'd notice more join in and before long the water below would go berserk with fish splashing and jumping out of the water. This usually continued for half and hour. It was a mad race to get a line and hook down there. But what sort of fish to go after? There were all sorts and sizes in that water.

We decided to work the food chain, so we put on some lightweight tackle. With the fish in a frenzy it wasn't long until we'd both hooked a small fish. We changed to a heavier line and hook and cast again.

My mate was so frustrated by the scores of fish jumping out of the water that he wanted to dive in and grab them with his bare hands. I'm thankful we were 20 ft up or he'd have given it a try. I checked out the little kid beside us who'd just caught a decent trevally on his hand line and resolved not to leave without a fish.

We dropped our lines. There were queenfish jumping everywhere and the baitfish were moving like a swarm

WHERE TO FISH

of locusts through the water. I hooked into something and the rod did the biggest arch I've ever seen.

I started winding but it was hard going and a huge haul before I could even see the fish. I kept going and the fish broke through the water. I reckoned it was a mangrove jack and I got all excited. I wound and wound but the fish wasn't giving in. Seconds later the line snapped, the rod flicked back, just missing my eye, and it was all over.

The pier is home to many skilled Aboriginal fishermen and I saw one of them below spear a great looking coral trout. I wasn't giving up. I got out my hand line. I was after the mangrove jack but I'd take anything. The kids was still reeling them in and Nana, an old Aboriginal lady, landed my mangrove jack.

In went the lines. Next minute my mate was tugging at his line, and a huge smile erupted on his face. I wanted to grab the line but I remembered I wasn't fishing with the kids or missus. It was a long haul but eventually a giant trevally broke through the water.

FISHING TIPS AND TALES

We fished the pier every day at the turn of the tides. By the end of the week I had bagged myself a coral trout, snapper, queenfish, trevally and, on the second last day, a mangrove jack. Yep, there's nothing wrong with good old-fashioned pier fishing.

TIPS FROM THE LOCALS

Locals are an invaluable resource when it comes to fishing, and you'll always find a character willing to share their experience and knowledge.

It was a local fisherman who told me the secret of live yabbies for yellow belly.

In Shark Bay, many years ago, an old pensioner showed me how to skin a small shark, my very proud catch for the day.

In Broome, an Aboriginal woman freely shared her knowledge about the local fish and what they liked, when they were likely to bite and how to catch something bigger and better. I listened, I learnt and I

WHERE TO FISH

passed on the information to the tourists who came by that week.

Sometimes the wisdom comes from locals but often it's from smart fishermen who are happy to share their secrets, like the generous bloke who told me to look for small birds on the water, which indicates a source of fish below. Or the cleaning lady who turned out to be an expert of whiting fishing (she heard a small piece of cuttlefish added to bait helps attract them).

When you go fishing and meet these characters, be open and accepting and you'll be the wiser for it.

MORE TIPS ON FINDING FISH

A good way to make your fishing trip harmonious is to know where and when to catch fish. Perhaps you'll find something in these tips.

- The best times to fish (on a daily basis) are at sunrise, sunset or tide changes. Also, the best fishing is said to occur three days before and three days after the new moon.

- The lowest tides occur when there's a full moon, and at that time it's easier to gather bait such as cunjevoi, mussels, pipis, yabbies and worms.

- Like snags, bridges are fish-holding structures and many are popular with anglers, particularly at night.

WHERE TO FISH

- Storms and strong fronts stir up water causing waves and currents that in time make food more readily available for fish. A rising barometer and a dying wind are good indicators that it's time to fish.

- Large-scale topographical maps are a good guide to accessible and remote areas for angling trips.

- Go to where there are fish. Sometimes familiar waters are not the best waters. A few hour's travel can often make the difference in the quality and size of the catch.

- Binoculars are handy in a boat for looking for schools of fish, working birds and other signs of fish activity.

- Echo sounders identify individual fish, bait schools, depths and fish-holding structures. As sounders cover a very small area at any one time they do not replace the skill and experience of a good angler.

- In very hot weather, native fish and trout tend to be found in deeper shady pools.

- Leaves, debris and lines of smooth water indicate wind lanes on lakes and impoundments. These are great places to troll and fish with lures and flies.

- Research the migratory paths of fish.

- For regular angling success fish the *edges* of deep and shallow water, reefs, warm and cold currents, weed beds, and fast and slow currents in rivers and streams.

- When parts of the ocean appear red in colour, it indicates a high concentration of shrimp-like creatures called krill. These concentrations attract large numbers of predators and so they are good places to fish.

- When angling, think positively. Tell yourself the target species is really in there and then

WHERE TO FISH

think of the most efficient way to produce a result.

- Hot-water outlets from power stations in the big cities offer excellent fishing.

- When arriving at a new fishing destination for the first time, call in to the local tackle shop. Most proprietors will put newcomers on the right track to a fish or two.

- A common belief is that dolphins frighten fish. This may be the case with some fish, but not all. Some can be caught by observing dolphin schools.

- Never ignore a floating clump of debris when fishing on the ocean. Nearly all debris has attendant bait schools and often predatory fish are not far away.

- Terns, garnets, cormorants and mutton birds are the best guides to fish schools as they actively pursue their food. Seagulls on the other hand often arrive to scavenge after the fish school has moved on.

- Underwater cameras are available commercially. Like radios, echo sounders and GPSs these cameras will reduce in price and increase in sophistication and will soon become common amongst boat owners.

WHERE TO FISH

GET THE FISH YOU WANT

In this section you'll find the top tips for catching whiting, snapper and barramundi.

HOW TO CATCH WHITING

- Success in fishing whiting requires patience, persistence and a certain exclusiveness of all other species.

- Be prepared to move from area to area in search of fish. Most reefy, weedy bays and estuaries contain good quantities of whiting.

- When fishing for whiting and other shallow-water fish, 20 minutes is long enough without a bite before moving to another area.

FISHING TIPS AND TALES

- Baits for whiting include pipis, mussels, squid, sandworms, yabbies and prawn pieces.

- The basic rigs for catching whiting are: the paternoster (a teardrop sinker, a leader of up to 60cm, and a No. 4 to 8 hook; the running sinker rig (a ball sinker, a stopper and a trace up to 60cm with a No. 4 to 8 hook); and the sinker to the hook rig (some anglers use a bright bead above the hook).

- Rods with fine tips are recommended, such as nibble tip or quiver tip.

- Use 2kg to 4kg braid or nylon lines. Braid is not recommended when constant snagging occurs.

HOW TO CATCH SNAPPER

- To find out the best spots to fish, listen to radio fishing sessions, follow press reports and

WHERE TO FISH

take note of the chat at fishing clubs and tackle shops.

- Be on the water and ready to fish as the sun rises or sets. These are the two best times regardless of tide changes.

- Have the freshest bait. Pilchard, garfish, squid, barracouta, sand whiting, sauries and fish fillets are all good baits. Dip pilchards and other bait in tuna oil as a scent attracter.

- Run a small ball sinker all the way to a No. 4/0 to 6/0 hook and use a 6kg to 10kg line.

- Set the reel with a drag of 1kg to 2kg and allow the fish to bend the rod tip to the water before firmly lifting the rod.

- Be patient and back your judgment. Changing areas can be unproductive and time wasting.

FISHING TIPS AND TALES

- Instead of using sounders try to find structures, holes and depth changes.

- Sea lice can demolish baits in minutes at night. A temporary solution is to attach a cork or a piece of foam above the bait to keep it off the bottom. If this doesn't work the only solution is to move to a new location.

- A large accumulation of boats can point out snapper schools; rather than trying to get a spot in the middle, join the outside of the group down current.

- Keep a yearly diary. The information gathered can be invaluable from season to season.

- Don't bully the hooked fish. Snapper are clean fighters and even the biggest fish can be captured if it's given its head when needed and pressure is applied carefully.

WHERE TO FISH

- Trim and discard the last 4m of line after each trip. Shellfish cuts can seriously weaken the breaking strain of the line.

HOW TO CATCH BARRAMUNDI

- While barramundi anglers love to see these spectacular fish jump, it often leads to lost fish. Some top barramundi guides exhort their clients to keep the rod tip down, even to put it under the water.

- Large barramundi ignore lures many times before suddenly striking. Patience is the key to trophy fish.

- Barramundi chase baitfish and prawns at the mouth of creeks and drains in the mangroves as the tide falls. Anchor or drift 20m off these features and cast with shallow running hard bodied lures. Spectacular action often occurs.

FISHING TIPS AND TALES

- When fishing for barramundi, listen for the distinctive 'boof' of a marauding fish.

- When fishing the tropical waters, locate the upper limit of tidal influence and work either side. This is where the fish will be.

- All large barramundi are female. To help preserve fish stocks of one of the world's most famous sport fish, take a photograph and quickly and gently release the fish.

PRACTICALITIES

RULES AND REGULATIONS

Fishing requires responsibility and adherence to rules and regulations that have been designed for the safety of everyone – not just fishermen, but the wider community. Regulations affect size and possession limits for a variety of fish species, fishing gear and much more. Make sure you know the rules and regulations relevant to where you want to fish, before you go fishing. Here are some general points:

FISHING TIPS AND TALES

- You must not use explosives, firearms, bows and arrows, spears, spearguns, or any projectile to take fish in inland waters.

- Excessive handling can damage a fish's body and slimy protective coating. If a fish is to be released, the hooks should be removed, if possible, while the fish is still in the water.

- Mammal blood and offal are not permitted for use as berley to attract fish.

- Fishing is prohibited in marine protected areas and to do so attracts hefty fines. When fishing a new location check with the local tackle store.

- Catch and size limits apply to may species of fish. Bag limits, boat limits, vehicle limits and possession limits are all types of catch limits. Fines are imposed for exceeding them.

- There are bans on catching some fish. These species are clearly identified in fishing guides

PRACTICALITIES

and where fishing licences are purchased.

- It's an offence to fillet some fish at sea.

- It is an offence, if you're not a licensed angler, to be in possession of an assembled rod, reel, and line at any inland water even if you're not fishing with it.

- Report illegal fishing activities, anonymously if you wish.

CARP

It is illegal to return noxious fish such as carp to the water. Put the carcasses to good use by burying them in the vegetable garden. Inform commercial harvesters about concentrations of carp and help keep the waterways open to more desirable species.

- If you catch a tagged fish record the date, length and location. Keep the tag, some scales and the fish or frame frozen and contact the relevant authority.

PRACTICALITIES

FISHING SAFETY

I'm rather partial to my body parts and I definitely don't like putting myself at unnecessary risk when I go fishing. Here are some practical tips on how to make your next fishing trip a lot safer.

BOAT FISHING

- Always brief new crew about life jackets, the radio, first aid kits and flares.

- If you're travelling by boat at night keep the speed down and stay alert for other craft, channel markers, sandbanks and floating debris.

FISHING TIPS AND TALES

- If you're fishing from a canoe or kayak you should have first learned the art of paddling and balancing.

- Steering the boat and setting the anchor can be a good distraction for those suffering seasickness.

- Battery problems and lack of fuel are the major causes of boating breakdowns. Always carry spares.

TACKLE

- Never release or break off a snagged lure or sinker with a direct pull. Anglers have been injured by a sudden release that sends the sinker or lure at them like a missile.

- Braid lines can cut fingers through to the bone. When you're snagged on a reef, wind the braid around a piece of soft pine timber (about the

PRACTICALITIES

size of a milk bottle); this will avoid broken rods, strained reel mechanisms and cut fingers.

FISH

- Some fish are venomous. Handle with extreme care and treat any new species with suspicion. Carry a pair of old garden secateurs to remove spikes.

- Relieve venomous fish stings with hot water. So where is hot water obtained at sea? That vacuum flask of hot coffee will do the job.

- Leatherjackets and toadfish have parrot like sharp teeth that can project beyond their jaws. It is far safer to leave the hook in these fish than try to retrieve it.

- Take special care with mako or blue pointer sharks. These fish can 'jump' aboard boats causing havoc. It's wise to leave them in the water until they are adequately noosed or gaffed.

THE ENVIRONMENT

- Fishing beneath trees can be hazardous as heavy limbs can drop with little warning.

- The sun can be fierce in an open boat. Use an umbrella to provide welcome shade. It may look strange but it is better than sunburn.

- Always wear a life jacket when crossing a coastal bar. The unexpected can happen at any time.

PRACTICALITIES

RELEASING FISH

These days, people are more inclined to release fish, especially those species that are threatened. That's a great thing; however, care must be taken or your good intentions may be wasted. Here are some tips for releasing fish.

- If you intend to release your fish, close the barbs on the single hooks or trebles. This will not affect the holding power of the hooks but will make catch and release much easier.

- In the marine world most large fish such as barramundi, flathead and bream are females. Releasing such large fish unharmed protects breeding stocks.

FISHING TIPS AND TALES

- Even though toadies and kelpfish are despised by anglers, they do have a place in the ecology. Releasing them unharmed is best for the environment.

- To revive fish that are brought to the boat or bank tired or exhausted, face them into the current and gently move them backwards and forwards, allowing water to pass through their gills

- Before handling a fish for release your hands should be wet. This protects the slime on the fish and ensures it will remain healthy.

- On releasing fish that swallow the hook, cut the line as near to the mouth as possible. The fish's stomach acids dissolve all but stainless steel hooks very quickly.

PRACTICALITIES

PREPARING FISH FOR THE TABLE

You've gone to all the hard work of catching your dinner. The last thing you want to do is spoil it. Here are some tips on keeping the catch fresh and preparing it for the table.

KEEPING THE CATCH FRESH

- Ice and salt water make an excellent slurry in which to keep the catch fresh and cool; as do bottles of frozen water.

- Salmon flesh can be improved if the fish are killed and bled on capture. Cut the fish through the gills and bend the head back. Bury the fish head-down in the sand or a bucket.

- Dusky morwong are targeted by spear fishermen and are occasionally caught on hook and line. The flesh is probably inedible and the fish should be returned live to the water. Sergeant baker has a similarly unpalatable flesh.

SCALING AND CLEANING

- Keeper nets can operate as 'scaling' bags for fish such as whiting, bream, flathead and garfish. Place the fish in the net and close the mouth of the net tightly. Tie with a rope to the boat's stern and tow at about 10 knots for 5 to 8 minutes. Presto! All the fish are scaled.

- If fish have to be cleaned at home in the kitchen, fill the sink with water and scale each fish beneath the surface.

- Scaling larger fish such as snapper or barramundi can be made much easier by using a long-handled scaler that's 60cm long. Place

PRACTICALITIES

the fish on a board underfoot and use two hands on the scaler to complete the task rapidly.

- Skinning or scaling fish is a matter of choice. Leatherjackets and sharks are always skinned before eating. As a rule, the tighter the scales, the more likely the fish will require scaling.

- Leatherjackets are the easiest of all fish to clean. Make a vertical knife-cut behind the spike, two-thirds of the way through the body. Pull the two parts apart. The head and gut come free in one piece. The remaining body is peeled like a banana and is ready for the table.

- Cleaning the black lining from the stomach cavity of luderick (and other fish with similar linings) is easy with a stiff nailbrush. For the fussy angler, a denture brush can get to the last corners.

FISHING TIPS AND TALES

- Cleaning elephant fish can be difficult. Remove the gut and trim all fins except the tail. Lay the fish flat and, beginning at the tail, remove a fillet from each side taking care not to cut through the soft cartilage backbone. Skin the fillet and slice finely for cooking.

- After being cleaned, squid develops a strong aroma. Separate it from other fish and keep it cold or frozen until use.

- If you intend to freeze fish such as salmon, kingfish and other species that contain concentrations of dark flesh it is a good idea to remove as much dark flesh as possible because it will turn black and the flavour will deteriorate.

HEALTH AND SAFETY

- Food poisoning from seafood can be severe. If in doubt, throw it out.

PRACTICALITIES

- When filleting fish, wear a filleting glove on the hand holding the fish. Professional fish handlers wear gloves as an occupational health and safety requirement.

- The most versatile filleting knife has a narrow flexible blade of around 18cm. Ordinary table knives with bone handles make great mussel opening knives. Short-bladed knives are used for opening oysters. Much larger knives are required for cleaning sharks, marlin and larger tuna.

FISHING TIPS AND TALES

HOW TO FILLET A FISH

Catching a fish is lots of fun but someone has to gut, clean and fillet it. Here's how to fillet a fish:

1. Cut an angle from behind the gill cage to the backbone on both sides of the fish.

2. Make another cut near the tail.

3. Slice open the belly, cutting as close to the backbone as possible.

4. Make a similar cut along the back, keeping close to the backbone.

5. Remove the flesh from the ribcage.

Tips

- Take your time and be gentle with the flesh.

PRACTICALITIES

- Make sure your knife is very sharp.

- Don't expect to end up with perfect fillets. You are merely removing the flesh from the bone.

- Be prepared to trim and clean up the fillet.

- A little bit of waste is better than spitting out bones.

RECIPES

FROM HOOK TO TABLE

Fishing is a great way to spend a day. It's a balm for the soul, a relaxing tonic for the mind and body. Creating a culinary masterpiece from the fish you've caught – or from the fish you've bought at your local fish market (after all, we fishermen throw many a threatened species back into the water), can be just as enjoyable and is a great way to extend the fishing trip even further. And, hey, a complete fishing guide wouldn't be complete without a few tasty recipes.

RECIPES

The two major complaints that people have about eating fish are that it tastes and smells 'fishy' and that its texture is unpleasant, ie tough, chewy, rubbery or soggy. The good news is, both of these complaints apply to old and improperly cooked fish, and both of these fish flaws can be avoided. A proper piece of fresh fish should smell sweet and briny, like the ocean. If you can detect a 'stinky fish' odor, then don't waste your money on it. Fish is highly perishable, and it is delicate. It should be cooked the day you buy it or catch it, but it can be stored for a day or two as long as you keep it very, very cold.

From trout in inland streams to deep blue ocean water species, fish and seafood are firm favourites on many dinner tables and barbeques. Baked, grilled, poached, smoked, fried, or steamed; appetizers, spreads, salads, or main course – seafood is healthy (especially important if your wife's watching your cholesterol!), easy to prepare (you can even watch the footy while you're doing it) and delicious (especially when washed down with a good beer – check out our very simple Beer Batter recipe a little later).

And if you're fishing for a few more good reasons to

FISHING TIPS AND TALES

eat it, how about these fabulous health benefits: fish is low in calories and saturated fat, high in vitamins, minerals and protein, and has been shown to reduce the risk of heart disease, depression and some kinds of cancer. Fish is your ticket to nutritional heaven!

Your tastebuds and your family — or your mates (depending on who you want to spend your Saturday night with!) — are in for a real treat. Even though we haven't given you tips earlier in this book on how to catch *all* of these beauties, don't let that stand in your way of a good feed. Get down to your fishmonger and ask him about his big catch. Who said living vicariously was no fun! And even if you'd normally choose prime rump steak over garlic poached trout, why not throw caution to the wind and captain the boat that is the stove. You'll turn yourself as well as your gilled friend into a great catch.

Don't forget to read *Preparing Fish for the Table* (page 227) for lots of practical tips on scaling, cleaning and filleting fish.

Here are some great recipes — enjoy!

What's in a Name?

Naming your dish is very important. A creative and unusual name will get attention. Descriptive words that capture the feeling of your dish add to its overall interest. For instance, say you're cooking fish for a special occasion. Instead of just serving it up, think about naming it 'Anniversary Chowder'. You get the idea.

Aussie Beer Batter Fish

Nothing could be simpler. Mix 2 cups plain flour, salt and pepper, and gradually add 310ml (10½ fl oz) beer. Dust 4 fish fillets with cornflour and coat with the batter. Cook in hot oil until golden brown. Drain on absorbent paper and serve with lemon wedges, tartare sauce and hot chips.

Do Not Overcook Your Fish

The most important thing to remember when cooking fish is not to overcook it. Fish cooks quickly and is the easiest of all meats to tell when it is done. You can tell by the color change, and watch the flesh change color as it cooks right to the middle. Often the flesh changes from translucent to opaque as it cooks. When grilling or frying, you may want to flip the portions to prevent overcooking one side. A good way to check is to break a piece in half or pry the flake with a fork to see if it has cooked all the way through. The fish is done when the color shift reaches the middle and it is the same color all the way through. Avoid giving it an extra minute or two for good measure.

Tips on how to Thaw Fish
- Thaw overnight in the refrigerator. Do NOT leave out on counter to thaw.
- Thin fillets and steaks will thaw within 8 to 10 hours in the refrigerator.
- Cook immediately after thawing.

SCALLOP PUFFS

preparation time
10 minutes

cooking time
20 minutes

nutritional value
fat: 10.3 g
carbohydrate: 22.4 g
protein: 8.7 g

Ingredients:

250 g (8 oz) sea scallops
4 tablespoons mayonnaise
60 g (2 oz) gruyère, freshly grated
½ teaspoon dijon mustard
1 teaspoon fresh lemon juice
1 tablespoon finely chopped fresh parsley
salt and pepper
1 large egg white
8 slices crusty white bread, toasted lightly, crusts discarded, and each slice cut into 4 squares
1 sheet puff pastry, cut into 25 squares (each 5 × 5 cm)

makes 32

1 Preheat oven to 160°C (315°F, gas mark 2–3). In a large pan combine scallops with enough salted water to cover completely, bring the water to a simmer, and poach scallops for 5 minutes. Drain well and cut into 1 cm pieces.

2 In a large bowl, whisk together mayonnaise, gruyère, mustard, lemon juice, parsley, salt and pepper, add scallops, and toss mixture well. In a small bowl, beat the egg white until it forms stiff peaks. Fold into scallop mixture gently but thoroughly.

3 Prick pastry squares with a fork and place on a lined oven tray. Bake for 5 minutes until lightly golden.

4 Preheat grill to medium high. Remove pastry from oven and place a heaped teaspoon of the scallop mixture onto each. Place under grill and cook until golden and bubbling.

SMOKED SALMON BITES

preparation time
10 minutes

cooking time
30 minutes

nutritional value per serve:
fat: 7.6 g
carbohydrate: 9.3 g
protein: 5.6 g

Ingredients:

16 small pontiac potatoes
4 tablespoons vegetable oil
250 g (8 oz) smoked salmon
½ cup (125 ml, 4 fl oz) sour cream
3 hard-boiled eggs, cut into small wedges
fresh dill sprigs
makes 32

1 Preheat oven to 180°C (350°F, gas mark 4). Cut potatoes into thick slices and place in a large bowl. Add oil and toss to coat well. Place potato slices on baking trays and bake for 30 minutes or until tender. Remove potatoes from oven and cool slightly.

2 To serve, top each potato slice with a little salmon, a teaspoon of sour cream, an egg wedge and a dill sprig. Serve warm.

SMOKED SALMON CARPACCIO

preparation time
15 minutes

nutritional value per serve
fat: 16.9 g
carbohydrate: 1.1 g
protein: 15.3 g

Ingredients:

4 tablespoons extra virgin olive oil
45 ml (1½ fl oz) lemon juice
1 small red onion, finely chopped
2 teaspoons small whole capers
350 g (11½ oz) smoked salmon
1 tablespoon roughly chopped parsley
black pepper, freshly ground
extra capers for garnish
serves 4

1 In a large bowl, combine oil, lemon juice, onion and capers. Whisk to combine and set aside.

2 Arrange smoked salmon on serving plates.

3 Drizzle the dressing over the smoked salmon, sprinkle with parsley and ground black pepper, and serve. Garnish with extra capers.

SALMON AND RICE NOODLES IN COCONUT SOUP

preparation time
25 minutes

cooking time
30 minutes

nutritional value per serve
fat: 8.1 g
carbohydrate: 3.9 g
protein: 4.5 g

Ingredients:

2 stalks lemon grass
2 cloves garlic, crushed
1 large onion, chopped
1 teaspoon ground turmeric
1 teaspoon ground hot chilli powder
1 tablespoon vegetable oil
400 ml (13 fl oz) can coconut milk
1¼ cups (315 ml, 10 fl oz) fish or chicken stock
250 g (8 oz) skinless salmon fillet, cut into 2.5 cm cubes
salt
125 g (4 oz) dried rice noodles
200 g (7 oz) fresh bean shoots
fresh coriander to garnish
1 lime, quartered, to serve
serves 4

1 Peel the outer layers from the lemon grass stalks and finely chop the lower white bulbous parts, discarding the fibrous tops. Place lemon grass, garlic, onion, turmeric and chilli powder in a blender and process to a coarse paste or grind with a pestle and mortar.

2 Heat the oil in a large, heavy-based pan. Fry the paste for 5 minutes until fragrant, stirring often. Add the coconut milk and stock, bring to the boil, stirring, reduce heat, cover and simmer for 15 minutes. Add the salmon and salt to taste, then simmer, covered, for 5 minutes or until fish has cooked through.

3 Cook noodles in a large pan of boiling water until al dente. Rinse well under cold water. Divide rice noodles and bean shoots between serving bowls and ladle over the salmon and coconut soup. Garnish with coriander and lime wedges.

HOT-AND-SOUR SCALLOP SOUP

preparation time
20 minutes

cooking time
25 minutes

nutritional value per serve
fat: 0.8 g
carbohydrate: 2.6 g
protein: 3.4 g

Ingredients:

1 litre (1⅔ pints) chicken broth
125 g (4 oz) mushrooms, thinly sliced
60 g (2 oz) bamboo shoots, sliced
250 g (8 oz) sea or bay scallops, sliced 5 mm thick
1 teaspoon soy sauce
¼ teaspoon white pepper
2 tablespoons cornflour
3 tablespoons warm water
1 egg, beaten
3 tablespoons rice vinegar
2 spring onions (green onions), thinly sliced

serves 4

1 Place chicken broth, mushrooms and bamboo shoots in a large pan. Bring to the boil, reduce heat and simmer 5 minutes. Rinse scallops under cold running water. Add scallops, soy sauce and pepper to the pan. Bring to the boil.

2 Combine cornflour and warm water. Add to the soup and stir until thickened. Stir briskly with a chopstick whilst gradually pouring in egg. Remove from heat. Stir in rice vinegar (white-wine vinegar may be substituted); sprinkle with spring onions. Serve immediately.

SMOKED TROUT RILLETES

preparation time
15 minutes, plus
30 minutes refrigeration

cooking time
10 minutes

nutritional value per serve
fat: 14.9 g
carbohydrate: 0.7 g
protein: 15.4 g

Ingredients:

240 g (7½ oz) smoked trout fillets
finely grated rind (zest) and juice of 1 lemon
2 tablespoons dry sherry
3 tablespoons butter, softened
extra 3 tablespoons butter, melted, for sealing (optional)
1 teaspoon capers, drained and chopped
extra capers to garnish (optional)
fresh herbs to garnish (optional)

serves 4

1 Into a large bowl, flake the fish, add lemon rind and juice, sherry, softened butter and capers, mixing well to combine. Alternatively, use a food processor or blender.

2 Spoon mixture into small bowls or ramekins. Pour over the melted butter, if using, and garnish with the herbs or capers, if using. Cover and refrigerate for 30 minutes or until the butter has set.

SCALLOP AND WATERCRESS SALAD

preparation time
25 minutes, plus
2 hours cooling and 1 hour refrigeration

cooking time
1 hour 35 minutes

nutritional value per serve
fat: 24.2 g
carbohydrate: 2.8 g
protein: 3.7g

Ingredients:

10 fresh scallops
90 g (3 oz) watercress; discard woody stems, select tender tips only
160 g (5½ oz) water chestnuts, halved
4 cherry tomatoes
50 g (1¾ oz) walnut halves
90 g (3 oz) bean shoots

dressing
⅔ cup (170 ml, 5½ fl oz) walnut or olive oil
2 tablespoons red-wine vinegar
2 small cloves garlic, crushed
salt and white pepper

serves 4

1 Combine dressing ingredients in a jar and shake well.

2 Place the scallops on a plate suitable for steaming. Sprinkle scallops with a little of the dressing and steam gently over boiling water for 6 minutes.

3 Snap watercress into 10 cm sections. In a large serving bowl, combine watercress, water chestnuts, cherry tomatoes, walnuts and bean shoots. Pour over the dressing and toss gently to coat well. Gently mix in the scallops and serve.

ANCHOVY, EGG AND PARMESAN SALAD

preparation time
10 minutes

cooking time
10 minutes

nutritional value per serve
fat: 5.0 g
carbohydrate: 0.6 g
protein: 3.7 g

Ingredients:

3 medium eggs
2 heads endive (chicory)
2 small butter lettuces, leaves torn
12 anchovy fillets in oil, drained and cut in half lengthways
1 tablespoon capers, drained
3 cherry tomatoes, halved
50 g (1¾ oz) parmesan cheese
3 tablespoons extra virgin olive oil
juice of 1 lemon
salt and black pepper
fresh flat-leaf parsley to garnish

serves 6

1 Bring a small pan of water to the boil, add eggs and boil for 10 minutes. Remove from pan, cool under cold running water, then shell. Cut each egg lengthways into quarters.

2 On each serving plate, arrange 8 alternating endive and lettuce leaves, tips facing outwards, in a star shape. Place 2 egg quarters on the base of 2 opposite lettuce leaves, then place 2 anchovy halves on the other 2 opposite lettuce leaves. Scatter the capers over the leaves.

3 Put a cherry tomato half in the centre of each plate and drape 2 anchovy halves over the top. Shave over the parmesan, using a vegetable peeler, then drizzle over the olive oil and lemon juice. Season to taste and garnish with parsley.

THAI FISH CAKES

preparation time
25 minutes

cooking time
10 minutes

nutritional value
fat: 14.7 g
carbohydrate: 2.5 g
protein: 11.3 g

Ingredients:

500 g (1 lb) boneless firm white fish fillets, skinned
3 spring onions (green onions), chopped
1 egg, lightly beaten
2 tablespoons plain flour
2 fresh red chillies, deseeded and chopped
½ teaspoon cumin seeds
2 teaspoons grated fresh ginger
vegetable oil for shallow-frying
coriander chutney
1 bunch fresh coriander
4 spring onions (green onions), chopped
1 tablespoon grated fresh ginger
1 clove garlic, crushed
2 tablespoons lime or lemon juice
1 tablespoon vegetable oil
serves 4–6

1 Place fish in a food processor and process until finely chopped. Add spring onions, egg, flour, chillies, cumin seeds and ginger and process to make a stiff paste.

2 Take 2 tablespoons of fish mixture and shape into a small flat cake. Place on a plate lined with plastic food wrap. Repeat with remaining mixture.

3 Heat oil in a frying pan over a medium heat and cook fish cakes in batches for 3–4 minutes each side or until cooked. Set aside and keep warm.

4 For the chutney: place coriander, spring onions, ginger, garlic, lime or lemon juice and oil in a food processor and process until smooth. Serve warm with fish cakes.

POTATO CAKES WITH SMOKED SALMON

preparation time
15 minutes

cooking time
40 minutes

nutritional value per serve
fat: 7.9 g
carbohydrate: 8.5 g
protein: 6.9 g

Ingredients:

300 g (10 oz) floury potatoes, unpeeled
150 ml (5 fl oz) milk
salt and black pepper
1 large egg
30 g (1 oz) plain flour
4 spring onions (green onions), finely sliced
1 tablespoon oil
½ cup (125 ml, 4 fl oz) crème fraîche
2 tablespoons chopped fresh dill
150 g (5 oz) smoked salmon slices
extra dill to garnish
lemon wedges to serve
serves 4

1 Cook the potatoes in boiling salted water for 15–20 minutes, until tender, drain. Cool for a few minutes, then peel. Mash with milk, season, then beat in the egg, flour and spring onions to make a batter.

2 Heat a large non-stick frying pan, add a little of the oil. Make 4 potato cakes, using 2 tablespoons of batter for each. Fry for 2–3 minutes on each side until golden. Drain on kitchen towels and keep warm while you make 2 further batches of 4 potato cakes.

3 Combine the crème fraîche and chopped dill. Serve pancakes topped with the salmon slices and a spoonful of crème fraîche. Garnish with black pepper, dill and lemon.

SMOKED SALMON SOUFFLÉS

preparation time
15 minutes

cooking time
35 minutes

nutritional value
fat: 20.4 g
carbohydrate: 3.1 g
protein: 13.4 g

Ingredients:

45 g (1½ oz) parmesan cheese
1 tablespoon butter
2 tablespoons plain flour
½ cup (125 ml, 4 fl oz) milk
4 tablespoons double cream
3 eggs, separated
60 g (2 oz) gruyère cheese, grated
60 g (2 oz) smoked salmon, shredded
1 tablespoon chopped fresh dill

serves 2

1 Grease 2 ramekins of 1 cup (250 ml, 8 fl oz) capacity and sprinkle base and sides with 30 g (1 oz) parmesan cheese.

2 Melt butter in a small pan over a medium heat. Stir in flour and cook for 2 minutes. Remove pan from heat and gradually whisk in milk and cream.

3 Return pan to heat and cook, stirring constantly, for 4 minutes or until sauce boils and thickens. Remove pan from heat and set aside to cool slightly.

4 Add egg yolks, gruyère cheese, remaining parmesan cheese, salmon and dill to sauce and mix to combine.

5 In a large bowl, place egg whites and beat until stiff peaks form. Fold egg white mixture into salmon mixture. Pour into ramekins and bake for 20–25 minutes or until soufflé are puffed and golden. Serve immediately.

SEARED TUNA WITH ROASTED PLUM TOMATOES

preparation time
20 minutes plus
30 minutes marinating

cooking time
30 minutes

nutritional value
fat: 21.6 g
carbohydrate: 1.7 g
protein: 5.1 g

Ingredients:

1 clove garlic, crushed
finely grated rind and juice of 1 lime
½ cup (125 ml, 4 fl oz) olive oil
3 tablespoons chopped fresh rosemary
4 (145 g, 5 oz) tuna steaks, about 2 cm thick
6 plum tomatoes, halved lengthways
1 red onion, halved and thinly sliced lengthways
salt and black pepper
extra olive oil for greasing
serves 4

1 Preheat barbecue to high. Preheat oven to 220°C (425°F, gas mark 7). In a large dish, combine garlic, lime rind, half the lime juice, 2 tablespoons of the oil and 1 tablespoon of the rosemary. Add the tuna and turn to coat evenly. Cover and refrigerate for 30 minutes.

2 Place the tomatoes and onion in a shallow ovenproof dish with the remaining rosemary. Drizzle with the remaining oil and season. Roast in the oven for 15–20 minutes, until tender and lightly browned.

3 Lightly oil barbecue grill bars. Place tuna on barbecue, cook for 4–5 minutes, turning once, or until golden. Serve with the tomatoes and onion, sprinkled with the remaining lime juice.

HOME COOKED TROUT

preparation time
15 minutes, plus
1 hour standing

cooking time
20 minutes

nutritional value
fat: 4.8 g
carbohydrate: 0.9 g
protein: 19.4 g

Ingredients:

125 g (4 oz) smoking chips
½ cup (125 ml, 4 fl oz) white wine
4 small rainbow trout, cleaned, with head and tail intact
1 tablespoon vegetable oil
3 red onions, thinly sliced
1 lemon, thinly sliced
8 sprigs dill
serves 4

1   Place smoking chips and wine in a large glass dish and stand for 1 hour.

2   Preheat covered barbecue to a low heat. Place smoking chips dish in barbecue over hot coals, cover barbecue with lid and heat for 5–10 minutes or until liquid is hot.

3   Place trout on a wire rack set in a roasting tin. Brush trout lightly with oil, then top with onions, lemon and dill. Place on rack in barbecue, cover and smoke for 15–20 minutes or until trout flakes when tested with fork.

CHAR-GRILLED TUNA WITH PEACH SALSA

preparation time
20 minutes, plus
1 hour refrigeration
cooking time
15 minutes
nutritional value
fat: 3.8 g
carbohydrate: 4.4 g
protein: 6.7 g

Ingredients:

4 (about 180 g, 6 oz) tuna steaks
1 tablespoon olive oil
fresh coriander chopped to garnish
lime wedges to serve
salsa
3 ripe peaches, peeled, stoned and finely chopped
4 spring onions (green onions), finely chopped
½ yellow capsicum (pepper), finely chopped
juice of ½ lime
1 tablespoon chopped fresh coriander
black pepper
serves 4

1 In a small bowl, place peaches, spring onions, capsicum, lime juice, coriander and black pepper and mix well. Cover and refrigerate for 1 hour.

2 Preheat the barbecue to high. Brush tuna steaks with oil and season with pepper. Place on barbecue and cook for 3–5 minutes on each side, until flesh flakes when tested with a fork. Garnish with fresh coriander and serve with the lime wedges and peach salsa.

FISHING TIPS AND TALES

SEAFOOD BARBECUE

preparation time
30 minutes, plus 20 minutes marinating

cooking time
30 minutes

nutritional value
fat: 1.1 g
carbohydrate: 6.9 g
protein: 9.2 g

Ingredients:

4 tablespoons soy sauce
2 tablespoons honey
2 tablespoons tomato sauce
2 tablespoons sesame seeds
1 tablespoon lemon rind (zest), finely grated
375 g (12 oz) green prawns, shelled and deveined, tails intact
250 g (8 oz) calamari (squid) rings
250 g (8 oz) boneless fish fillets, cut into thick strips
4 potatoes, thinly sliced
4 small tomatoes, halved
2 tablespoons chopped fresh thyme
freshly ground black pepper
lemon or lime wedges
serves 4

1 Preheat barbecue to a high heat. In a large shallow glass dish, place soy sauce, honey, tomato sauce, sesame seeds and lemon rind. Add prawns, calamari and fish, toss to coat, cover and refrigerate for 20 minutes.

2 Sprinkle potatoes and tomatoes with thyme and black pepper to taste. Cook potatoes and tomatoes on a well-oiled barbecue plate for 10 minutes or until potatoes are crisp and tomatoes soft. Push vegetables to the side of the barbecue to keep warm.

3 Add seafood mixture to barbecue and cook, turning frequently, for 5 minutes or until cooked. Serve vegetables and seafood garnished with lemon or lime wedges.

LEMON AND HERB-BASTED SCALLOPS

preparation time
30 minutes

cooking time
15 minutes

nutritional value
fat: 8.3 g
carbohydrate: 1.8 g
protein: 7.7 g

Ingredients:

4 tablespoons butter, melted
2 tablespoons lemon juice
1 clove garlic, crushed
1 teaspoon finely chopped fresh basil
1 teaspoon finely chopped fresh coriander
1 teaspoon finely chopped fresh mint
500 g (1 lb) fresh scallops
1 red onion, cut into wedges
1 red capsicum (pepper), cut into triangles
watercress for garnish
lemon wedges to serve
8–10 metal skewers
serves 6

1 Preheat barbecue plate to high. In a small bowl, combine the butter, lemon juice, garlic and herbs, and set aside.

2 Thread scallops, onion and capsicum onto skewers, brushing each skewer with butter mixture.

3 Place skewers onto barbecue and cook for 4–5 minutes, turning once and brushing with remaining butter mixture, until scallops are tender. Serve garnished with watercress and lemon wedges.

CAPSICUM-BARBECUED WHOLE SNAPPER WITH GHERKIN MAYONNAISE RELISH

preparation time
10–15 minutes

cooking time
25–40 minutes

nutritional value
fat: 6.3 g
carbohydrate: 3.5 g
protein: 15.8 g

Ingredients:

1 whole snapper (1.5 kg, 3 lb)
3 tablespoons chopped red capsicum (pepper)
2 teaspoons chopped fresh basil
2 tablespoons lemon juice
1 tablespoon olive oil
gherkin mayonnaise
250 g (8 oz) mayonnaise
90 g (3 oz) gherkins, chopped
serves 4

1 Prepare kettle/weber for cooking or preheat barbecue to high. Cut and scale the fish and rinse well. Pat dry with paper towels.

2 In a small bowl, combine capsicum, basil, lemon juice and oil. Spoon some into the cavity of the fish and spread the remainder over the fish.

3 Lay the fish on a large sheet of oiled foil and roll up the edges to seal the fish, leaving the top of the fish exposed. Place fish on the grill bars in kettle/weber or hooded gas barbecue and cook for 35–40 minutes or until fish flakes when tested with a fork.

RECIPES

JAPANESE MARINATED SALMON, CUCUMBER AND DAIKON SALAD

preparation time
30 minutes, plus 2 hours marinating
nutritional value per serve
fat: 3.4 g
carbohydrate: 1.8 g
protein: 8.8 g

Ingredients:

700 g (1 lb 7 oz) fillet salmon, centre cut
6 tablespoons mirin
3 tablespoons soy sauce
1 tablespoon grated fresh ginger
1 teaspoon sesame oil
1 continental cucumber, washed
1 teaspoon sea salt
1 tablespoon castor sugar
3 tablespoons rice vinegar
1 endive (curly chicory)
1 daikon (japanese white radish), finely julienned
serves 6–8

1 Using an extremely sharp knife, slice the salmon very thinly placing the knife at an angle. Place the slices neatly in a flat based dish.

2 Whisk together mirin, soy, ginger and sesame oil then remove 2 tablespoons and reserve. Pour the remainder over the sliced salmon and cover with plastic wrap. Place in the refrigerator to marinate for 2 hours.

3 Using a potato peeler or food slicer cut the cucumber into long, thin ribbons from each side avoiding the seeds. Break chicory into bite-sized pieces and in a large bowl toss together with cucumber and daikon. Mix together the sea salt, sugar and rice vinegar and toss through the salad.

4 Pile the endive salad into the centre of individual entrée plates or a large platter and arrange the marinated salmon around the edge. Drizzle reserved mirin over the salad.

LIME FISH WITH NOODLES

preparation time
10 minutes

cooking time
5 minutes

nutritional value per serve
fat: 1.9 g
carbohydrate: 5.2 g
protein: 11.3 g

Ingredients:

2 teaspoons vegetable oil
3 spring onions (green onions), chopped
1 stalk fresh lemon grass, chopped or ½ teaspoon dried lemon grass, soaked in hot water until soft
1 fresh red chilli, chopped
750 g (1½ lb) firm white fish fillets, cut into thick strips
2 tablespoons lime juice
315 g (10 oz) fresh rice noodles
½ bunch (250 g, 8 oz) bok choy (pak choi), chopped
4 tablespoons water
2 tablespoons soy sauce
2 teaspoons white miso

serves 4

1 Heat wok over a high heat, add the oil, spring onions, lemon grass and chilli and stir-fry for 1 minute. Add fish and lime juice and stir-fry for 2 minutes or until fish is almost cooked. Remove fish mixture from wok and set aside.

2 Add noodles, bok choy, water, soy sauce and miso to wok and stir-fry for 2 minutes. Return fish mixture to wok and stir-fry for 1 minute or until heated through

ORIENTAL-STYLE SALMON FILLETS

preparation time
5 minutes,
plus 30 minutes marinating

cooking time
8 minutes

nutritional value per serve
fat: 11 g
carbohydrate: 8.5 g
protein: 13.7 g

Ingredients:

4 skinless salmon fillets
2 tablespoons vegetable oil
2 tablespoons light soy sauce
2 tablespoons clear honey
25 g (1 oz) stem ginger, drained and finely chopped
2 spring onions (green onions), cut into long strips
finely grated rind (zest) and juice of ½ lime
black pepper
lime wedges to serve
serves 4

1 Place the salmon fillets in a shallow non-metallic dish. Mix together the oil, soy sauce, honey, ginger, spring onions, lime rind and juice and seasoning. Pour over the fillets and turn to coat. Cover and marinate in the refrigerator for 30 minutes to 1 hour.

2 Preheat the grill to high. Lightly oil a baking tray. Lift the fillets and spring onions out of the marinade and place on the baking tray. Brush the fillets with a little of the marinade, then cook for 3 minutes. Turn over, brush with more of the marinade and grill for 3–5 minutes until cooked through. Garnish with lime wedges.

FRAGRANT SALMON STIR-FRY

preparation time
10 minutes, 2 hours marinating

cooking time
10 minutes

nutritional value per serve
fat: 12.6 g
carbohydrate: 2.5 g
protein: 11.2 g

Ingredients:

250 g (8 oz) skinless salmon fillets
1½ tablespoons peanut or sunflower oil
1 tablespoon chilled butter, cubed

marinade
1 stalk lemon grass
1 tablespoon soy sauce
½ cup (125 ml, 4 fl oz) orange juice
1 tablespoon chopped fresh dill
1 tablespoon chopped fresh basil
1 teaspoon grated fresh root ginger
1 clove garlic, crushed
salt and black pepper

serves 2

1 Peel the outer layer from the lemon grass stalk, then finely chop the lower white bulbous part. In a bowl, combine lemon grass, soy sauce, orange juice, ½ tablespoon dill, ½ tablespoon basil, ginger, garlic and seasoning. Cut the salmon fillet into strips 2.5 cm wide and 7.5 cm long. Arrange strips in a shallow non-metallic dish and pour over marinade, turning strips to coat. Cover and refrigerate for 2 hours.

2 Remove salmon from dish and set aside the marinade. Pat salmon dry. Heat the oil in a large, heavy-based frying pan over a medium to high heat, add salmon and cook for 2 minutes on each side.

3 Arrange salmon on serving plates. Pour reserved marinade into the frying pan, bring to the boil and simmer for 2 minutes. Whisk in butter, a cube at a time. Spoon sauce over the salmon and sprinkle over remaining dill and basil.

RECIPES

THAI STICKS WITH CUCUMBER SALAD

preparation time
25 minutes

cooking time
6 minutes

nutritional value per serve
fat: 2.6 g
carbohydrate: 8.3 g
protein: 9.4 g

Ingredients:

salad
1 cucumber, peeled and thinly sliced
4 tablespoons white-wine vinegar
4 tablespoons white sugar
1 large red or green chilli, deseeded and finely chopped
1 small spring onion (green onion), thinly sliced

fish sticks
small handful fresh coriander
4 spring onions, chopped
450 g (14 oz) cod or other skinless white fish fillet, cubed
3 tablespoons red curry paste
1 teaspoon salt
2 teaspoons lime juice
1 large egg white
12 stalks lemon grass

serves 4

1 Combine cucumber, vinegar, sugar, chilli and 1 small spring onion with 4 tablespoons of cold water. Cover and set aside in a cool place.

2 Place coriander and remaining spring onions in a food processor and process until finely chopped. Add fish, curry paste, salt and lime juice and process until the fish is finely chopped. Add egg white and continue processing until the mixture is stiff.

3 Divide the fish mixture into 12 portions, then carefully press each around a lemon grass stick, forming a 'sausage' shape. Preheat the grill to high. Place the fish sticks on a lightly oiled baking sheet and grill for 6 minutes, turning once, until cooked and lightly browned on all sides. Serve with the cucumber salad.

JAPANESE PRAWN AND VEGETABLE TEMPURA

preparation time
25 minutes, plus 20 minutes standing

cooking time
10 minutes

nutritional value per serve
fat: 1.4 g
carbohydrate: 19 g
protein: 7.2 g

Ingredients:

1 zucchini (courgette)
salt
4 green prawns
1 red capsicum (pepper)
1 large egg
150 g (5 oz) plain flour
½ cup (125 ml, 4 fl oz) ice-cold water
peanut oil for deep-frying
lime wedges to serve
soy sauce to serve
serves 4

1 Cut the zucchini in half across the centre, trim the end and cut each half lengthways into 4. Sprinkle with salt and set aside for 20 minutes. Shell the prawns, leaving tails attached. Devein, using a sharp knife. Rinse and refrigerate. Deseed the capsicum and cut into 8 strips.

2 Break the egg into a mixing bowl. Mix in the ice-cold water and fold in the flour to make a lumpy batter.

3 Heat 5 cm of oil in a wok or frying pan. Coat the zucchini slices in batter and deep-fry for 3 minutes or until golden, turning halfway through. Drain on kitchen towels and keep warm. Repeat with capsicum strips. Coat prawns and cook for 1 minute. Serve immediately with lime wedges and soy sauce.

BAKED PENNE WITH TOMATOES AND ANCHOVIES

preparation time
20 minutes

cooking time
40 minutes

nutritional value per serve
fat: 17.4 g
carbohydrate: 25 g
protein: 12.9 g

Ingredients:

250 g (8 oz) ripe tomatoes
250 g (8 oz) mozzarella, grated
4 tablespoons grated parmesan
55 g (2 oz) cheddar, grated
2 tablespoons dried oregano
4 tablespoons extra virgin olive oil, plus extra for greasing and drizzling
salt and black pepper
2 tablespoons butter
1 small onion, finely chopped
2 garlic cloves, crushed
400 g (13 oz) dried penne
4 anchovy fillets, drained and chopped

serves 4

1 Preheat oven to 200°C (400°F, gas mark 6). Put tomatoes into a bowl, cover with boiling water. Leave for 30 seconds, peel, deseed and chop. Combine mozzarella, parmesan, cheddar, oregano, 2 tablespoons of oil and season. Set aside.

2 Heat remaining oil and butter in a frying pan. Add onion and cook for 5–7 minutes, until softened. Add garlic, cook for 1 minute. Add tomatoes, season with salt, cook for 5 minutes until tomatoes have softened.

3 Cook pasta in a large pan of boiling water, until al dente. Drain well, toss through tomato sauce. Grease a deep ovenproof dish and spread 2–3 tablespoons of the cheese mixture and half the anchovies over the base. Top with pasta, cover with the remaining anchovies and cheese mixture. Drizzle with olive oil, bake in the oven for 15–20 minutes, until golden.

SPAGHETTINI AND SCALLOPS WITH BREADCRUMBS

preparation time
10 minutes

cooking time
15 minutes

nutritional value per serve
fat: 13.7 g
carbohydrate: 35 g
protein: 8.5 g

Ingredients:

400 g (13 oz) dried spaghettini
12 fresh scallops with their corals
½ cup (125 ml, 4 fl oz) extra virgin olive oil
50 g (2 oz) fresh breadcrumbs
4 tablespoons chopped flat-leaf parsley
2 cloves garlic, crushed
1 teaspoon dried chillies, crushed
½ cup (125 ml, 4 fl oz) dry white wine

serves 4

1 Cook spaghettini in a large pan of boiling water, until al dente. Drain well and set aside.

2 Detach corals from scallops and set aside. Slice scallops into 3 or 4 pieces. Heat 2 tablespoons of oil in a frying pan, add breadcrumbs and fry, stirring, until golden. Remove from pan and set aside.

3 Heat remaining oil in the pan, add 2 tablespoons of parsley, the garlic and chilli. Cook for 2 minutes.

4 Add scallops and cook for 30 seconds, until starting to turn opaque. Add wine and the reserved corals, cook for a further 30 seconds, add spaghettini and cook for 1 minute, tossing to heat through. Sprinkle with breadcrumbs and remaining parsley.

TAGLIATELLE WITH TOMATO AND MUSSELS

preparation time
30 minutes

cooking time
1 hour 15 minutes

nutritional value per serve
fat: 1.7 g
carbohydrate: 17 g
protein: 5.6 g

Ingredients:

400 g (13 oz) dried tagliatelle
225 g (7½ oz) cooked shelled mussels
2 tablespoons chopped fresh basil extra basil, for garnish

sauce
750 g (1 lb 8 oz) plum tomatoes
1 tablespoon olive oil
1 onion, finely chopped
2 cloves garlic, crushed
2 sticks celery, finely chopped
1 red capsicum (pepper), chopped
125 g (4 oz) button mushrooms, finely chopped
4 sun–dried tomatoes, finely chopped
½ cup (125 ml, 4 fl oz) red wine
2 tablespoons tomato puree
black pepper

serves 4

1 To make sauce, cover plum tomatoes with boiling water and leave for 30 seconds. Drain, peel, deseed and chop.

2 Heat oil in a pan. Add onion, garlic, celery, red capsicum and mushrooms. Cook for 5 minutes until softened, stirring occasionally. Add chopped tomatoes, sun-dried tomatoes, red wine, tomato puree and black pepper. Bring to the boil, cover, reduce heat and simmer for 20 minutes or until vegetables are tender, stirring occasionally.

3 Cook the tagliatelle in boiling water, until al dente. Add mussels to tomato sauce, increase heat and cook, uncovered, for 5 minutes, stirring occasionally. Drain pasta, add to sauce with basil, toss well. Garnish with basil leaves and serve.

SPAGHETTI WITH TUNA

preparation time
15 minutes

cooking time
40 minutes

nutritional value per serve
fat: 7.5 g
carbohydrate: 25 g
protein: 9.1 g

Ingredients:

3 tablespoons extra virgin olive oil
1 onion, chopped
2 cloves garlic, crushed
6 anchovy fillets, drained
400 g (13 oz) can chopped tomatoes
185 g (6 oz) can tuna chunks in olive oil, drained and flaked
black pepper
400 g (13 oz) dried spaghetti
3 tablespoons chopped flat-leaf parsley

serves 4

1 Heat oil in a large frying pan, gently cook onion for 5–7 minutes, until softened. Add garlic and anchovies, cook for 2 minutes until anchovies have broken down.

2 Increase heat, stir in tomatoes and simmer, uncovered, for 5 minutes. Add tuna and pepper. Mix well, reduce heat and simmer for 20–25 minutes, until sauce has thickened.

3 Cook the pasta in a large pan of boiling water, until al dente. Drain well. Transfer to a serving bowl, spoon over the sauce and toss well. Garnish with parsley.

LINGUINI WITH PRAWNS AND SCALLOPS

preparation time
15 minutes

cooking time
55 minutes

nutritional value per serve
fat: 3.8 g
carbohydrate: 12 g
protein: 7.9 g

Ingredients:

400 g (13 oz) linguine
1 kg (2 lb) tomatoes
olive oil, for drizzling
salt and pepper
90 ml (3 fl oz) olive oil
220 g (7½ oz) scallops
220 g (7½ oz) green
    prawns, peeled
150 g (5 oz) calamari
    (squid), cut into rings
220 g (7½ oz) firm white
    fish fillet, cut into cubes
3 garlic cloves, crushed
2 brown onions, chopped
1 tablespoon tomato paste,
    optional
⅓ cup (90 ml, 3 fl oz)
    water
2 tablespoons chopped
    fresh parsley
parmesan, grated
serves 4

1 Preheat oven to 180°C (350°F, gas mark 4).

2 Cook linguine in a large pan of boiling water, until al dente. Drain, set aside and keep warm. Cut the tomatoes in half and place on a baking tray. Drizzle with olive oil, sprinkle with salt and pepper, and roast in oven for 40–45 minutes.

3 Place in a food processor and process until just combined.

4 Heat oil in a large pan, sauté onion and garlic until lightly coloured. Add fish, tossing gently for 1–2 minutes. Add calamari, cook 1 minute, add scallops and prawns, cook a further minute. Add tomato mixture, tomato paste and water and simmer for 5–10 minutes, making sure not to over cook seafood. Season with salt and pepper, stir through parsley. Serve with linguine and garnish with parmesan.

BAKED RIGATONI WITH SMOKED SALMON

preparation time
15 minutes

cooking time
30 minutes

nutritional value per serve
fat: 16.3 g
carbohydrate: 24 g
protein: 14.2 g

Ingredients:

400 g (13 oz) dried rigatoni (pasta tubes)
salt
150 g (5 oz) gruyère, grated
150 g (5 oz) cheddar, grated
2 tablespoons chopped fresh dill
200 ml (7 fl oz) crème fraîche
½ teaspoon cayenne pepper
2 tablespoons butter
250 g (8 oz) smoked salmon, cut into strips

serves 4

1 Preheat oven to 200°C (400°F, gas mark 6). Cook pasta in boiling water, until al dente. Drain, return to pan. Set aside 1 tablespoon each of the gruyère, cheddar and dill. Combine rest with the pasta, crème fraîche and cayenne.

2 Grease a 20 × 15 cm ovenproof dish with half the butter, spoon in half the pasta. Lay salmon strips on top and cover with remaining pasta. Sprinkle with reserved gruyère, cheddar and dill, then dot with the remaining butter. Cover with foil, bake for 15 minutes. Remove foil and bake for a further 5 minutes or until the top is bubbling and golden.

LOBSTER LEMON AND DILL SAUCE

preparation time
15 minutes

cooking time
20 minutes

nutritional value per serve
fat: 15.2 g
carbohydrate: 23 g
protein: 8.3 g

Ingredients:

500 g (1 lb) spaghetti
4 green lobster tails
90 g (3 oz) butter
1 clove garlic, crushed
½ cup (125 ml, 4 fl oz) sherry
2 tablespoons chopped fresh dill
155 ml (5 fl oz) fish stock
350 ml (11½ fl oz) cream
1 tablespoon tomato paste
salt to taste
freshly ground black pepper
juice of ½ lemon
extra fresh dill, chopped
serves 4

1 Cook spaghetti in a large pan of boiling water, until al dente. Drain, set aside and keep warm.

2 Remove lobster meat from shell and cut into medallions.

3 Melt butter in a frying pan and sauté garlic for 1 minute. Add lobster and sauté for 1–2 minutes. Remove from pan, set aside and keep warm.

4 Add sherry and dill to frying pan. Cook until liquid is reduced by half. Add fish stock, again reducing by half. Reduce heat, add cream, tomato paste, salt and pepper and simmer for 4–5 minutes.

5 Return lobster meat and juices to pan, add lemon juice and combine to heat through. Serve on spaghetti, garnish with extra dill.

CHINESE-STYLE STEAMED GREY MULLET

preparation time
10 minutes,
plus 30 minutes refrigeration

cooking time
20 minutes

nutritional value per serve
fat: 8.8 g
carbohydrate: 0.8 g
protein: 15.4 g

Ingredients:

- 1 grey mullet, about 700 g (1 lb 7 oz), scaled and gutted
- ½ teaspoon salt
- 1 tablespoon vegetable oil
- 1 tablespoon light soy sauce
- 1 large carrot, cut into fine strips
- 4 spring onions (green onions), cut into fine strips
- 1 tablespoon grated fresh root ginger
- 1 tablespoon sesame oil (optional)
- fresh coriander to garnish

serves 2

1 In a small bowl, combine salt, vegetable oil and soy sauce. Make 4 deep slashes along each side of the fish, and rub inside and out with the sauce mixture. Cover and place in the refrigerator for 30 minutes.

2 Spread half the carrot, spring onions and ginger in the centre of a large piece of foil. Place the fish on top, then sprinkle with the remaining vegetables and ginger and any remaining oil mixture.

3 Loosely fold over the foil and seal. Transfer the fish to a steamer or a rack set over a roasting tin half filled with water. Cover the steamer tightly with a lid or the roasting pan with foil. Cook for 20 minutes or until the fish is firm and cooked through. Put the sesame oil, if using, into a small saucepan and heat. Drizzle over the fish and garnish with coriander.

TIGER PRAWN, SNOW PEA AND MANGO STIR-FRY

preparation time
15 minutes
cooking time
5 minutes
nutritional value per serve
fat: 3.6 g
carbohydrate: 4.2 g
protein: 8.6 g

Ingredients:

400 g (13 oz) green tiger prawns, peeled
2 tablespoons vegetable oil
1 ½ tablespoons finely grated fresh root ginger
300 g (10 oz) snow peas (mangetout)
bunch of spring onions (green onions), sliced
1 large ripe mango, peeled and thinly sliced
2 tablespoons light soy sauce

serves 4

1 Cut a slit along the back of each prawn with a sharp knife and remove any thin black vein.

2 Heat the wok on a high heat, add oil, ginger and prawns and stir-fry for 2 minutes or until the prawns are just turning pink. Add the snow peas and spring onions and stir-fry for a further minute to soften slightly. Stir in the mango and soy sauce and stir-fry for 1 minute to heat through. Serve with steamed rice.

THAI FISH CAKES WITH PEANUT DIPPING SAUCE

preparation time
20 minutes

cooking time
16 minutes

nutritional value per serve
fat: 16.9 g
carbohydrate: 7.5 g
protein: 9.8 g

Ingredients:

350 g (11½ oz) skinless cod fillets
1 tablespoon thai red curry paste
1 tablespoon thai fish sauce
2 tablespoons cornflour
1 medium egg, beaten
1 spring onion (green onion), finely chopped
60 g (2 oz) fine green beans, cut into 5 mm lengths
peanut oil for shallow-frying
dipping sauce
2 tablespoons sugar
juice of 1 lime
1 clove garlic, finely chopped
1 cm piece fresh root ginger, finely chopped
1 tablespoon roughly crushed roasted salted peanuts
1 small red chilli, deseeded and finely chopped
2 tablespoons light soy sauce

serves 4

1 In a food processor, finely mince the cod fillets. Add red curry paste, fish sauce, cornflour and egg. Blend briefly or stir until mixed. Transfer to a bowl and combine with spring onions and beans.

2 Lightly oil your hands (it's quite sticky), then divide mixture and shape into 8 patties. In a bowl, combine sugar and lime juice, stirring until sugar dissolves. Stir in garlic, ginger, peanuts, chilli and soy sauce. Set aside.

3 Heat 1 cm of oil in a large frying pan over a medium to high heat, then fry half of the fish cakes for 3–4 minutes on each side, until golden. Drain on kitchen paper, then cook remaining cakes. Serve with dipping sauce.

BAKED COD WITH GINGER AND SPRING ONIONS

preparation time
10 minutes

cooking time
25 minutes

nutritional value per serve
fat: 1.4 g
carbohydrate: 0.6 g
protein: 15.1 g

Ingredients:

oil for greasing
500 g (1 lb) piece cod fillet
1 tablespoon light soy sauce
1 tablespoon rice wine or medium-dry sherry
1 teaspoon sesame oil
salt
3 spring onions (green onions), shredded and cut into 2.5 cm pieces, white and green parts separated
2.5 cm piece fresh root ginger, finely chopped

serves 4

1 Preheat the oven to 190°C (375°F, gas mark 5). Line a shallow baking tray with a piece of lightly greased foil to come past the sides of the baking tray. Place the cod on the tray, skin-side down. Pour over the soy sauce, rice wine or sherry, oil and salt to taste, then sprinkle over white spring onion and ginger.

2 Loosely wrap the foil over the fish, folding the edges together to seal. Bake for 20–25 minutes, until cooked through and tender. Unwrap the parcel, transfer the fish to a serving plate and sprinkle over spring onions.

PRAWN JABALAYA

preparation time
20 minutes

cooking time
43 minutes

nutritional value per serve
fat: 0.8 g
carbohydrate: 8.6 g
protein: 7.9 g

Ingredients:

- 3 rashers bacon, cut into strips
- 1 large onion, finely chopped
- 1 green capsicum (pepper), diced
- 1 celery stalk, chopped
- 3 cloves garlic, crushed
- 1 cup (200 g, 7 oz) long-grain rice
- 440 g (14 oz) can tomatoes
- 2 cups (500 ml, 16 fl oz) chicken stock, boiling
- 2 teaspoons cajun spice mix
- 1 teaspoon dried thyme
- 500 g (1 lb) green medium prawns, shelled and de-veined
- 155 g (5 oz) smoked ham in one piece, cut into 1 cm cubes
- 2 spring onions (green onions), finely chopped

serves 4

1 Cook bacon in a frying pan over a medium heat for 5 minutes or until crisp. Remove bacon from pan and drain on absorbent paper.

2 Add onion to pan and cook, stirring, for 5 minutes or until onion is soft, but not brown. Add capsicum, celery and garlic and cook for 3 minutes. Add rice and cook, stirring frequently, for 5 minutes or until rice becomes translucent. Add the tomatoes and their juices; slash through with a knife to break up. Stir in stock, spice mix and thyme and bring to the boil. Cover, reduce heat to low and cook for 15 minutes.

3 Stir in prawns and ham, cover and cook for a further 10 minutes or until rice is tender and liquid absorbed. Sprinkle with crisp bacon and spring onions and serve immediately.

LOBSTER PROVENÇALE

preparation time
15 minutes

cooking time
15 minutes

nutritional value per serve
fat: 4.2 g
carbohydrate: 20 g
protein: 10.3 g

Ingredients:

- 1¼ cups (250 g, 8 oz) long-grain rice
- 4 tablespoons butter
- 1 teaspoon freshly crushed garlic
- 2 spring onions (green onions), chopped
- 310 g (10 oz) canned tomatoes, chopped
- salt and cracked black peppercorns
- pinch of saffron
- 1 large cooked lobster or 4 cooked lobster tails
- 4 tablespoons brandy
- ½ bunch fresh chives, chopped, for garnish
- 1 lemon

serves 4

1 Boil the rice 12–13 minutes or until tender, drain and keep hot. In a shallow frying pan, melt butter over a moderate heat. Add garlic, spring onions, tomatoes, salt, pepper and saffron. Cook about 2 minutes until onions are translucent.

2 Remove meat from lobster and cut into large pieces. Add lobster meat to pan and flame with the brandy. Cook gently until lobster is heated through.

3 On serving plate, place rice and sprinkle with chives. Arrange the lobster on the rice and spoon over the sauce from the pan. Serve with lemon wedges.

SEAFOOD PAELLA

preparation time
15 minutes

cooking time
45 minutes

nutritional value per serve
fat: 3.1 g
carbohydrate: 9.4 g
protein: 8.3 g

Ingredients:

1 tablespoon olive oil
2 onions, chopped
2 cloves garlic, crushed
375 g (12 oz) long-grain white rice
1 litre (1⅔ pints) chicken stock
pinch saffron threads
250 g (8 oz) calamari (squid) rings
185 g (6 oz) smoked ham, sliced
250 g (8 oz) chorizo sausage, sliced
440 g (14 oz) can peeled tomatoes, undrained and mashed
315 g (10 oz) white fish fillets, cubed
250 g (8 oz) green medium-sized prawns, shelled and de-veined
500 g (1 lb) mussels, scrubbed and beards removed
125 g (4 oz) peas

serves 6

1 In a paella pan or large deep-frying pan, heat oil over a medium heat. Add onions and garlic and cook, stirring, for 3 minutes, until onions are soft. Add rice and cook, stirring, for 4–5 minutes until rice is translucent.

2 Stir stock, saffron, calamari, ham, sausage and tomatoes into pan and bring to the boil. Reduce heat and simmer, stirring occasionally, for 25 minutes or until rice is tender and liquid is absorbed.

3 Place fish, prawns, mussels and peas on top of rice mixture, add a little extra hot stock or water if needed. Reduce heat to low, cover and cook for 10 minutes or until seafood and peas are cooked. Discard any mussels that do not open after 5 minutes. Serve immediately.

STIR-FRIED TAMARIND PRAWNS

preparation time
20 minutes, plus
20 minutes standing

cooking time
10 minutes

nutritional value per serve
fat: 2.3 g
carbohydrate: 6.9 g
protein: 9.8 g

Ingredients:

- 2 tablespoons tamarind pulp
- ½ cup (125 ml, 4 fl oz) water
- 2 teaspoons vegetable oil
- 3 stalks fresh lemon grass, chopped, or 2 teaspoons finely grated lemon rind (zest)
- 2 fresh red chillies, chopped
- 500 g (1 lb) medium green prawns, shelled and deveined, tails intact
- 2 green (unripe) mangoes, peeled and thinly sliced
- 3 tablespoons chopped fresh coriander leaves
- 2 tablespoons brown sugar
- 2 tablespoons lime juice

serves 4

1 In a bowl, place tamarind pulp and water and stand for 20 minutes. Strain, reserve liquid and set aside. Discard solids. Heat oil in a wok or frying pan over a high heat. Add lemon grass or lemon rind and chillies and stir-fry for 1 minute. Add prawns and stir-fry for 2 minutes or until they change colour.

2 Add mangoes, coriander, sugar, lime juice and tamarind liquid and stir-fry for 5 minutes or until prawns are cooked.

SICHUAN-STYLE SCALLOPS

preparation time
8 minutes

cooking time
5 minutes

nutritional value per serve
fat: 3.2 g
carbohydrate: 15.6 g
protein: 5.7 g

Ingredients:

1½ tablespoons peanut oil
1 tablespoon finely chopped ginger
1 tablespoon finely chopped garlic
2 tablespoons finely chopped spring onions (green onions)
500 g (1 lb) scallops, including corals
steamed rice to serve
mint dressing
1 tablespoon rice wine or dry sherry
2 teaspoons light soy sauce
2 teaspoons dark soy sauce
2 tablespoons chilli bean sauce
2 teaspoons tomato paste
1 teaspoon sugar
2 teaspoons sesame oil
serves 4

1 Heat wok until very hot. Add the oil and when it is very hot add the ginger, garlic and spring onions. Stir-fry for 10 seconds. Add the scallops and stir-fry for 1 minute.

2 In a bowl, combine the rice wine or sherry, soy sauces, chilli bean sauce, tomato paste and sugar. Add to the scallops. Stir-fry for 4 minutes until the scallops are firm and thoroughly coated with the sauce.

3 Add the sesame oil and stir-fry for 1 minute. Serve at once with steamed rice.

DEEP-FRIED CHILLI FISH

preparation time
8 minutes, plus
30 minutes marinating

cooking time
14 minutes

nutritional value per serve
fat: 3.9 g
carbohydrate: 11 g
protein: 13.7 g

Ingredients:

2 × 500 g (1 lb) whole fish such as ream, snapper, whiting, sea perch, cod or haddock, scaled and gutted
4 red chillies, chopped
4 fresh coriander roots
3 cloves garlic, crushed
1 teaspoon black peppercorns, crushed
vegetable oil for deep-frying
red chilli sauce
⅔ cup (170 g, 5½ oz) sugar
8 fresh red chillies, sliced
4 red or golden shallots, sliced
⅓ cup (90 ml, 3 fl oz) coconut vinegar
⅓ cup (90 ml, 3 fl oz) water

serves 2–4

1 Make diagonal slashes along both sides of the fish. In a food processor, place chopped chillies, coriander roots, garlic and black peppercorns and process to make a paste. Spread mixture over both sides of fish and marinate for 30 minutes.

2 In a saucepan, place the sugar, sliced chillies, shallots, vinegar and water. Cook, stirring, over a low heat until sugar dissolves. Bring mixture to simmering and simmer, stirring occasionally, for 4 minutes or until sauce thickens.

3 Heat vegetable oil in a wok or deep-frying pan until a cube of bread dropped in browns in 50 seconds. Cook fish, one at a time, for 2 minutes each side or until crisp and flesh flakes when tested with a fork. Drain on absorbent kitchen paper. Serve with chilli sauce.

FINAL WORD

So, that's fishing! I hope you enjoyed the journey as much as I did. I'm heading up to Broome for a well-deserved rest. I'm going fishing in my new boat – second-hand from a bloke who didn't use it enough. It's not big enough to do anything else in but fish, but I don't mind. If I get all five members of my family on it at the same time, I'll be a lucky person, but I'll take what comes.

I'm going back after my mangrove jack. It's not only a superb fish to eat; it's also lots of fun to catch. It is one of the most powerful fish to fight and when it's on the end of your line you'd think it's three times its actual

FINAL WORD

size. They usually grow from 1kg to 3kg, but they can reach 10kg. The Australian record is 11.679kg.

The mangrove jack is attracted to snaggy areas of submerged trees and mangrove roots along the edge of estuaries, rivers and tidal creeks. It is a tough sport fish that pulls hard when hooked and uses cover for its advantage.

Floating live bait near a fallen tree or sunken tree works well, or trolling or casting near snags. It's best to set the hook and retrieve some line immediately because the little blighters bite and run. Moving the bait produces more strikes and trolling strip baits instead of lures can help keep the cost of lost lures down to a minimum.

If I have no luck I'm going back to the pier.

Happy fishing!

Lee Vernon